PERMISSION TO
thrive

my journey from grief to growth

SUSAN ANGEL MILLER

Permission to Thrive: My Journey from Grief to Growth
© 2019 by Susan Angel Miller

Published in the United States by LRS Press
www.susanangelmiller@gmail.com

Library of Congress Cataloging-in-Publication Data are available upon request.

Paperback ISBN: 978-1-7324960-3-3 (p)
Printed in the United States of America

Book design by Robin Krauss, www.lindendesign.biz
Cover design by Kathi Dunn, www.dunn-design.com
Editor: Erika DeSimone, www.erikasediting.com

This book is dedicated to Laura.

For her curiosity, motivation, and kindness.

For teaching me to embrace life.

For embedding herself in our hearts.

Lola

Contents

I Am

By Laura Miller, age thirteen.
Inspired by Mitch Albom's *The Five People You Meet in Heaven*.

I am vivacious and motivated
I wonder what I will accomplish in the years to come
I hear the stars twinkling at midnight
I see people sitting on clouds of fluff in the sky
I want to be an editor-in-chief of a fashion magazine
I am vivacious and motivated

I pretend to live in the future
I feel like I want to be the world's repairman
I touch the horizon, wondering what the future will be like
I worry about the consequences that humanity might face
I cry for all the people whose voices are not heard
I am vivacious and motivated

I understand that life is too short
I say that we should all be ourselves
I dream of making a large impact in society
I hope that we can appreciate how fortunate we are
I am vivacious and motivated

June 1, 2008

Part I
From Grief to Growth

Prologue

M om, my head is pounding!" Laura exclaimed. It was mid-January 2009, and she'd been in her room studying for an exam. This wasn't the first time she'd complained of a headache over the last few weeks, but because she was a high-achieving and somewhat anxious student, I'd attributed Laura's headaches to stress. Teenage hormones, a consistently too-heavy backpack, the demands of her freshman year of high school, or the chlorine in her school's swimming pool all seemed likely causes as well. Yet now, after her third complaint, I decided it was time to call her doctor, who recommended Tylenol and told me to call back if the headaches persisted.

The headaches did persist, though, and over the next few weeks, they became both longer-lasting and more painful. I did my best to soothe and care for Laura when her pain surged. I tried to tell myself that headaches are common; I tried to remind myself that her pediatrician hadn't seemed overly concerned. But when, in mid-February, Laura called me from the school nurse's office, my mouth went dry. "Mom, my head hurts so much," she complained with an intensity I wasn't used to hearing from her. "Can you pick me up?"

I scheduled a doctor's appointment for the next day, Friday the 13th. When her neurological exam was complete, the doctor called me into the room. I saw Laura sitting on the exam table, swinging her legs and smiling. "I'm feeling much better, Mom," she assured me. The doctor announced that the headaches were probably stress related. I breathed a sigh of relief.

Laura woke up with another headache the next day, yet she insisted on attending a recruitment event at her Jewish youth group that evening. She treasured her friendships with the teens in her BBYO chapter, and she was looking forward to meeting the younger recruits and encouraging them to join. My husband Ron and I debated if we should allow her to go, but we didn't have the heart to say no.

With the doctor's recent reassuring words echoing in my head, going about our weekend as planned seemed the right thing to do. On Sunday, Ron helped Laura with her science fair project, while I kept myself busy by arranging the details of our second daughter Sara's *bat mitzvah*, which was in two weeks and would be attended by more than one-hundred and fifty guests.

Still, I couldn't shake my growing unease or my looming sense of powerlessness, and I could tell that Ron—who is generally cool and levelheaded—was also starting to worry. In my gut I knew something was "off," but at the same time I trusted that our life as a family would continue on in the same safe, protected way it always had.

CHAPTER 1

The Promised Land

Be kind. Act with integrity. Avoid controversy. Write thank-you notes. Follow the rules. These were among the principles that my parents ingrained in me as a child, and by living these values, I believed my adult life would be as trouble-free as my childhood had been.

Predictability was a constant in my young life. Growing up in Evanston (a suburb of Chicago), my father Jack held the same job as an accountant for as long as I could remember; he was a devoted volunteer leader at our synagogue. My mother did some volunteer work as well, but otherwise she was a stay-at-home mom until I was in high school. When she did return to work, it was in the counseling department at my school.

There were six of us in our home—my parents, my older sister Karen and my younger brother Steven, and my maternal grandmother (who lived with us until I was nine years old). We were close, and my parents valued family above all else. Although I didn't have any first cousins, my immediate family and I celebrated holidays with my great-aunts and great-uncles as well as my second and third cousins. Each summer we took a road trip to Pennsylvania to visit my paternal grandparents as well. These family get-togethers and summer trips are still some of my most vivid and cherished childhood memories.

My upbringing was idyllic in the sense that my parents unselfishly focused on our well-being and—in their actions as much as their words—they clearly imparted their values and expectations for the three of us. I had no desire to rebel, and I remember taking pride in trying to live up to my last name, Angel. My biggest "childhood crisis" was a bicycle accident when I was eleven years old. As I darted across the street on my bike, a passing car plowed into me, propelling me over the hood and onto the cement road. Even as I lay on the pavement, I remember being upset with myself for not having looked both ways as I'd been taught. After a three-day hospital stay, I spent the remaining summer months recovering from badly bruised legs as well as my ego.

My parents valued education and encouraged us to pursue careers that appealed to us but were also practical. When my father insisted I take a typing course the summer before I started high school, I wasn't surprised and didn't object. "If you know how to type, you'll always have a job," he advised. His guidance suited my good-girl, middle-child, peacemaker mentality.

Much of my self-esteem stemmed from the respect and praise I received from my parents and teachers, and I looked forward to the start of each school week. The first student I met in high school was Michelle, a girl with short brown hair and glasses. We introduced ourselves and then compared typing speeds. That night, I pulled my diary out of its hiding place and made a list of our similarities and differences: Michelle seemed smart, I was a good student; we both played the piano; my parents were married, hers were divorced; we were Jewish, her family wasn't. I weighed the pros and cons and, in the end, decided to give friendship with her a try.

Michelle would soon play a pivotal role in the beginning of my future family. During a class break one morning, she introduced me to her new friend Ron, who was in a class down the hall. I immediately sensed his self-confidence, and I was attracted to his olive complexion, straight brown hair, and slim build. My friendship with Ron gradually developed through our work on the debate team and the school newspaper. In the middle of our senior year, as we were returning from an out-of-town debate tournament, we found ourselves holding hands.

Ron expanded how I perceived the world. He taught me that I could confront and negotiate difficult situations without being seen as rude or antagonistic. He encouraged me to challenge myself and become more assertive. He gave me confidence and taught me that—no matter what I put my mind to—I was as capable as anybody else, if not more so. He was dependable, intelligent, easy to talk to, and he accepted me for who I was.

Our college years separated us by distance—I was at the University of Michigan, Ron at the University of Pennsylvania—and there were many times during college when I missed being with him. Despite our different paths, we stayed together and saw each other during semester breaks and occasional weekend visits. We both dated a few other people at times, yet, for me, no one matched the comfort, friendship, and attraction I felt when I was with Ron.

In February of our senior year, Ron accepted an investment-banking job offer in New York City. After graduation we moved to Manhattan, and I found an administrative position where I was able to use the French-language skills that I'd learned during my study-abroad semester in Aix-en-Provence. Ron and I saw each other almost every day, but we lived in two separate apartments, and paid two separate rents, to avoid disappointing our parents by living together before marriage.

Ron proposed to me nine months after we graduated from college. We were married just a few weeks shy of my twenty-fourth birthday in a Jewish ceremony in our hometown. Because I trusted so intrinsically in our relationship, I worried more about tripping over my long dress as I walked down the aisle than whether or not I was marrying the right guy. With him at my side, I believed my adult life would resemble the stability and predictability of my childhood.

We make a good team. Ron's a cynical optimist who has almost infinite patience . . . right up until his "I've reached the end of my rope" moment. Although we share the same values, we act as foils for each other: he's a list-maker, I'm not; he works with numbers, I prefer words; he focuses on available information and makes gut-level decisions, I consider all options in the hope of finding the one "right" answer. Ron functions at a higher speed and with more efficiency than I do, and even today I still remind myself that we're not competing for some illusive prize, that we each possess our own strengths. We both know we're stronger together than apart, and I'm thankful we're on the same team.

Not quite six months after our wedding, we returned to Evanston. After Ron earned his graduate business degree from Northwestern University, he took a position as a corporate banker in Chicago. I worked at a bank consulting firm and took graduate business classes in the evenings. Two years later (around the time I was completing my MBA), I resigned from my job before launching my own marketing consulting business.

Soon after I began working for myself, Ron was offered an investment banking job in Milwaukee. Ninety miles north of Chicago, Milwaukee seemed like a good fit for us. We both appreciated Midwestern values, and after seeing the tree-lined streets that hugged familiar Lake Michigan, we immediately felt at home. We liked the idea of being close enough to visit our families, yet far enough away to be independent.

After six years of marriage, at Thanksgiving dinner, Ron and I joyfully announced we were expecting. Life was progressing as planned; we were both meaningfully employed, becoming involved in Milwaukee's Jewish community, healthy, and about to begin a family.

As a newborn in 1994, Laura wasn't an easy baby. She needed us in a way that our younger two daughters wouldn't in the years to come. We held her baby-naming ceremony eight days after her birth (the same time frame as is mandated for a boy's circumcision) in our home, with friends and family surrounding us. Laura, as usual, was fidgety and fussy, and I comforted her as my college roommate Barbara, who'd recently been ordained as a rabbi, recited her blessings. On most nights, Laura fell asleep snuggled next to us in our bed before we carried her into her own room—as first-time parents, we were too naive and enamored to know the importance of creating a consistent sleep-schedule. During the day, Laura demanded, through her insistent and purposeful crying, that I carry her around the house, upright and over my shoulder, so she could observe the world with her inquisitive blue eyes. We had expected, in those early months, that her eyes would darken to a brown, like mine and Ron's, but they never did—they remained blue like her grandfather Marvin's.

I adored Laura and loved being a mom, but the long days of breastfeeding, diapering, and infant care exhausted and overwhelmed me. I envied other new moms whose babies slept for several hours each afternoon, which gave them a much-needed break. Laura, however, did no such thing. She disliked being alone—even though "alone" meant I never was any farther away than the next room. I wondered how single moms, or those without enough emotional support or resources, were able to manage the everyday stresses.

With the assistance of various college-aged babysitters, I juggled my consulting business with the responsibilities of motherhood. Ron supported me as best he could, but he worked long hours and sometimes didn't arrive home until after 10:00 p.m. As Laura's primary weekday caretaker, I often felt depleted— Laura seemed to thrive on attention in the way other babies thrived on formula. I remember one evening in particular when I thrust our daughter into Ron's arms as soon as he came home from work; escaping into the darkness, I took a walk around the block to calm myself.

When Sara was born two years later, she would sleep in her portable car seat contented, and Ron and I were amazed at how much less attention, even as a newborn, she needed than her older sister. We loved and nurtured Sara, even as Laura— precocious and verbal at an early age—continued to demand our main focus. She soaked up our hugs with joy and delighted in our adult conversations. Mature for her age, Laura loved telling "dramatic" stories, which I remember more as coherent tales than as a toddler's babbling.

Sara's birth marked a tipping point. With a newborn and a two-year-old, I couldn't keep up with both work and family. I quickly tired of racing home after client appointments, swapping out my work clothes for sweatpants before rushing to relieve the babysitter. Although I wrestled with the idea of sacrificing my career goals, not using my MBA skills, and assuming a more traditional role at home, I ultimately decided to phase out my consulting and instead concentrate my full attention on parenting our daughters.

Soon after I became a mom, our local Jewish Community

Center (JCC) grew to be my primary vehicle for making friends—starting with Laura's weekly "Tot Shabbat" classes. I made "mom friends" there, but our conversations mostly revolved around our children's feeding schedules. I enjoyed these conversations, yet I still craved a circle of adults whose main concern wasn't diapers.

Growing up, and until moving to Milwaukee, I hadn't viewed Judaism as a social or professional outlet. But now that I needed some adult-focused time, I contacted the local National Council of Jewish Women (NCJW)—an organization my mother had been involved with—with the goal of volunteering a few hours each week. The president treated me to lunch and told me of a board opportunity for the upcoming term. I readily accepted. I focused my efforts on increasing membership, as well as on early childhood education and domestic violence prevention. I didn't intend to take on a leadership role beyond being on the board, but soon enough (due to a shortage of willing volunteers), I found myself installed as co-president. I shared the position with five other board members, the majority of whom were much older than me.

Volunteering was exactly what I needed. I was using my marketing skills within the community, yet I was still able to retain the flexibility to parent my daughters in the way I'd always envisioned. I next accepted a board position with the JCC, and then I also became involved in the Women's Division of the Milwaukee Jewish Federation (MJF). In these roles, I met women and men who shared their wisdom, insights, and values, and who welcomed our family into Milwaukee's close-knit Jewish community. Around the same time I began volunteering, Ron did, too. In addition to getting involved at our synagogue, he took on leadership positions in local business groups. As our volunteering increased, so did our community network of friends and contacts.

When Laura was five years old and Sara was three, the birth of Rachel, our beautiful youngest daughter, completed our family. Taking care of three children under the age of five was wonderful, but also hectic and draining. I remember one night I was so thoroughly exhausted that I fell asleep sitting up, spilling a full glass of water on myself in the process!

As Rachel got a little older, our lives became more of a juggling act than ever. Ron still worked long hours, and since my volunteering had become more like an unpaid full-time job, I often relied on babysitters so I could attend lunchtime meetings and evening events. Once Rachel entered kindergarten, though, I was able to arrange my schedule so I could be home with Laura, Sara, and Rachel in the afternoons. After school each day, I would spend the hours before dinner with them, often in the kitchen, as they ate their snacks, worked on their art projects, or did their homework. I listened as they each told me about the "exciting details" of their days, and we all shared our thoughts and opinions with each other. I also had the "pleasure" of refereeing occasional sibling quarrels as well as chauffeuring them to piano, gymnastics, and tennis lessons.

During these hectic, rollercoaster days, we showed our love for each other with "I love yous" and random hugs. "Sandwich kisses," where Ron and I would position one of our girls between us and (on cue) kiss her on opposite cheeks, were a family favorite. These kisses often turned into contests where we would "compete" to give the longest one. (Ron almost always won.) Most nights we also cuddled with Laura, Sara, and Rachel in our king-size bed, and, as each child went to her own room for the night, Ron's tuck-in routines led to shrieks and giggles.

Our weekends were sometimes as hectic as our weekdays. With our desire to pass down Jewish traditions from generation to generation, *l'dor v'dor*, we enrolled our girls, each at the earliest possible age, in our synagogue's Sunday school program; as each of them entered the third grade, they began attending Hebrew school weekly as well. Although we didn't regularly observe *Shabbat*, we did sometimes attend Friday night and/or Saturday morning services. We also observed Passover, the High Holidays, *Hanukkah*, and other Jewish celebrations.

Yet for all the daily stresses, our family was healthy and strong, with little more than the normal bumps and bruises along the way. Ron and I were grateful. As parents, we were doing everything we thought we were "supposed to do," and I believed that following that path would serve us well as a family, would somehow safeguard us.

CHAPTER 2

In One Single Day

February 18, 2009

The Tuesday night following her doctor's appointment, Laura crawled into bed with me. I'd been trying to rationalize away my unease since Friday, but her headaches were worsening. So were my fears. Ron had left on a business trip Sunday night, and although I wished he were home, I was glad to let Laura sleep beside me if it would bring her some comfort.

Before she fell asleep, I placed warm, moistened washcloths under her neck and shoulders. I really didn't know what else to do to relieve her pain; I felt powerless against her unrelenting headaches. Tylenol wasn't helping anymore, and until I could take her back to her doctor, I was at a loss. Laura tossed and turned throughout the night.

In the morning while I was brushing my teeth, I heard Laura vomit several times, something which she'd never done before. Terror gripped me. I ran to her and comforted her, gathered up the soiled bedclothes, spread out a fresh sheet, and then lay her back down. She moaned and asked what was happening. "Don't worry about throwing up," I assured her as I put on my bravest face, "it's going to be okay."

Downstairs in the kitchen, I toasted waffles for Sara and

Rachel. Laura called for me. She needed the restroom and asked for my help. Once we were in the bathroom, she looked at me, clearly scared and puzzled. "Mom, why do you have four eyes?" she asked. My entire body stiffened.

Trying to avoid letting my fear show, I guided her down the hallway toward my bedroom, reassuring her as we walked. I planned to get her settled then immediately call her doctor. Suddenly, halfway down the hall, Laura collapsed into my arms. Her body became rigid, her hands curled awkwardly against her body, and her eyes rolled back into her head. I yelled for Sara to bring me the phone before I even knew I was screaming.

Within minutes, I heard the wailing of a siren. Sara and Rachel called upstairs to tell me an ambulance had pulled into the driveway. Two paramedics ran up the stairs and immediately slipped an oxygen mask over Laura's face.

Laura opened her eyes and asked what was happening. "Don't worry, it's going to be all right," I replied, this time with a forced confidence. I didn't know what was happening, either.

The paramedics carried Laura downstairs on a stretcher. I switched into controlled-confusion mode—I said a rushed goodbye to Sara and Rachel, grabbed my purse and phone, then hurried after the paramedics. Before I climbed into the ambulance's front seat, a neighbor assured me she'd get Sara and Rachel off to school. As we pulled away from the house, I told the driver how worried I was. "Don't worry," he calmly responded. "There's a bad stomach virus going around. Just about anything can cause a seizure in kids."

I called Ron, who was several hours away and in the middle of a meeting. He listened without interrupting, then asked if he should come home; I told him to wait until after I talked to the doctors. Then I phoned the event planner for Sara's *bat mitzvah* and canceled my late-morning appointment. As we raced to the hospital, selecting centerpieces no longer mattered.

From the front seat, I could hear Laura talking with the paramedics. She sounded like her usual chatty self, and I allowed myself to relax a bit. Maybe the driver had been right; maybe there was a commonplace cause for this frightening episode.

When we arrived at the pediatric hospital, and after she'd been moved to a curtained-off area of the emergency room, Laura told me how nice the paramedics had been to her. "We should send them a thank-you note," she said. "That's a really nice idea," I replied, proud of, but not surprised by, her gratitude and thoughtfulness.

While a nurse was changing her into a hospital gown, Laura began to hyperventilate. As she breathed into a brown paper bag, I noticed that her left wrist was still bent and frozen into a claw-like position. I didn't know if Laura realized this too; I hoped not. I wished Ron were with me.

Thirty minutes later, Laura was wheeled down the hallway for a CT scan. A nurse handed me a protective lead vest so I could stay in the room during the scan. From twenty feet away, I watched as Laura was maneuvered into the large, doughnut-shaped machine. The technicians huddled in their glass-paneled booth as they examined the scans on their screens. They avoided looking at me.

Laura was brought back to the curtained-off area, where she was given both morphine and an anti-anxiety medicine; she began drifting in and out of sleep. Waiting for the CT results by myself was too much, so I dialed my good friend Ruth—she dropped everything and arrived as fast as she could. We sat beside each other, next to Laura's bed, and shared a sandwich as we waited to learn more. Looking back, I'm surprised I was able to eat at all.

An emergency-room doctor soon appeared. "Your daughter has an aggressive mass in the back of her brain, in her cerebellum," she reported. "The tumor is increasing her intracranial pressure." This was the cause of Laura's headaches; the vomiting, double vision, and seizure were all results of the pressure having reached a critical point. The tumor would have to be removed, and quickly. An MRI scan, now scheduled for the afternoon, would tell us more. The doctor left as abruptly as she'd arrived.

I couldn't seem to get enough air into my lungs, but I forced myself to breathe. Slumped in my chair, I stared at Ruth. "I can't believe this is happening," I gasped. Ruth said something reassuring in reply, but I don't remember her exact words. As I tried to compose myself, I announced numbly, "It'll be all right," as if to convince myself. I could barely grasp the gravity of Laura's diagnosis. More to myself than to Ruth, I repeated, "It's going to be benign, and she'll be fine."

Laura would be all right, she *had* to be. I was utterly incapable of considering any other possibility. Her tumor would be removed, and our lives would resume as before. That's how things always worked in our family. This morning would just be one bad day in a string of many good future ones.

I believed in this outcome so unquestioningly that—I'm embarrassed to admit—one of my first thoughts was whether we would have to cancel Sara's *bat mitzvah*. When I'd awoken that morning, I had been in party-planning mode, but now I didn't know if we could still host Sara's long-awaited celebration; I didn't know if Laura would be recovered enough to come home, or if I would need to be with her in the hospital. The only thing I was sure of was that we'd deal with this crisis as a family—just as we'd plowed through other obstacles—and that, like in the past, everything would be fine in the end.

I clung to that belief. When Laura's pediatrician arrived at the hospital, she confirmed the CT results. I believed—and desperately hoped—that Laura was too groggy to overhear or understand us. If she'd heard, I knew she would begin asking countless questions to me about the procedures and her prognosis. She'd be frightened by the uncertainty and the risks, yet I wouldn't have any answers to give her—at least not yet. Plus, worrying was my job, not Laura's. I didn't want her to worry at all. Period.

Later that afternoon, I followed as an orderly rolled Laura, still in her bed, to radiology. In the hallway, doctors and nurses streamed past me with focus and purpose, oblivious to my rising panic. It was a typical workday for them, whereas for me any sense of normalcy had disintegrated into dread.

Sitting in a nearby chair, I was barely able to watch as Laura was lifted onto the MRI's sliding table and maneuvered into the machine's narrow tube. When the MRI's earsplitting banging began, the noise overwhelmed me; I clamped my hands over my ears with clenched fists, then escaped to a nearby waiting room. I was glad Laura had been fitted with earplugs; hopefully the banging wasn't too frightening for her.

The pediatric neurosurgeon found me a little while later and delivered the MRI's results. He was optimistic: Laura's tumor was encapsulated and not attached to her brain stem, which meant he could remove it. "Friday is the first day we have an operating room available. That's when she'll have the surgery," he said. His report was in-line with my beliefs—her tumor would be removed, it would be benign, and things would return to normal. Friday was little more than thirty-six hours away. Thirty-six more hours and my daughter would be fine.

I called Ron, who'd left his meeting and was now driving back to Milwaukee, to tell him the encouraging news. He assured me that Laura would be all right, but his optimism was muted. I appreciated his calmness but, at the same time, I knew he hadn't lived the terror of the last seven hours. When he asked about Sara and Rachel, I told him our friend Margie had agreed to stay with them overnight. "I'll meet you at the hospital after I pick up Sara and Rachel and get them settled at home," he promised.

As I walked to Laura's new semi-private room, a nurse handed me a bag full of the clothes Laura had been wearing when she was admitted. I reached into the bag and grabbed her T-shirt, which she'd received on her trip to Washington, D.C. the year before. I scrunched it up and tossed it into a trash barrel, hoping to banish any reminders of the morning.

Ruth stayed with me as Laura alternated between drug-induced sleep and short waking periods. I couldn't quite understand how the child lying in bed before me was the same girl who shared her secrets with me late at night, and who always walked beside me—holding my hand—even when Ron, Sara, and Rachel were five paces ahead. How could this be the same girl who dreamed of someday being the editor in chief at *Vogue*?

Ron arrived at about 7:00 p.m., and he hugged me tightly before we turned our full attention to our daughter. An hour or so later, he told me to go get something to eat in the cafeteria downstairs—he would stay with Laura. I wasn't at all hungry, but I hadn't eaten since before noon, and I realized my body would need fuel for the evening and overnight hours. I appreciated Ron's common sense and concern for me.

Twenty minutes later, after forcing myself to eat a yogurt, I returned to Laura's floor. As the elevator doors opened, I saw Ron sprinting down the hallway toward the nurses' station. My mouth went dry. While I was downstairs, Laura's pain had become excruciating: Ron had pushed the emergency call button several times without getting a response. He'd now managed to grab the nurses' attention, but they could do little to help—they needed to locate an attending doctor to authorize more pain medicine. I hesitated briefly outside Laura's half-open door and listened in anguish as she cried, "My head hurts, my head hurts!"

Ron and I were helpless. We stood by Laura's bed telling her how much we loved her. We tried to soothe her, but her cries continued. It seemed an eternity before a doctor finally arrived. He prescribed a new medicine for the pain, which a nurse quickly inserted into Laura's IV. We breathed a sigh of relief as her pain seemed to subside, but in the next moments, red and purple blotches began appearing on her face and arms. There was nothing Ron and I could do but stand back as the nurse injected another medicine to reverse the allergic reaction. I was screaming inside yet frozen—Laura's condition was deteriorating faster than I could take in. How was this happening?

The room went silent. A few seconds passed.

"She's not breathing!" a nurse yelled. She pushed the code-blue button. Emergency lights flashed and alarms blared. Doctors and nurses flooded into the room to resuscitate and stabilize our daughter.

The medical team began moving Laura's bed toward the door. Ron and I didn't know where they were taking her. "The tumor's putting too much pressure on her brain. We're bringing her to the operating room to insert a shunt!" one doctor shouted to us. In shocked confusion, we followed as nurses rolled Laura into the elevator. An oxygen mask covered her mouth: I couldn't tell if she was breathing on her own.

With Laura now in surgery, Ron and I were told to head down a dimly lit hallway to the waiting area. Chairs lined the perimeter of the empty room, and a children's plastic play set lay in the middle of the floor. We sat down and stared at each other incredulously: Laura had woken up at home this morning, she'd been in school only yesterday, and—with the exception of her headaches—she'd been her normal, healthy, motivated self. Yet now she was undergoing an invasive brain procedure. We couldn't believe what was happening to her—or to us.

Ron ran his hand through his hair. I looked away before I shut my eyes and placed my head in my hands. We waited. A chaplain joined us. She sat across from us and listened to our swirling questions and concerns about Laura's care: What if she'd been placed in intensive care instead of in a regular room? What if the doctors hadn't underestimated her condition? What if she hadn't been allergic to the pain medicine? What if they'd relieved the pressure in her brain sooner? What if they'd given her more attention? Laura had received more attention in the last twenty minutes than in the last six hours, and we believed her condition never should've reached such a crisis point. In one single day, Laura had gone from bad to worse too fast for any of it to make any sense. The chaplain was kind, but she had no answers.

The surgeon emerged from behind the swinging doors, his head lowered. "The procedure went fine, but Laura's neurological status isn't improving as we'd like." He was concerned that her brain had been damaged from a lack of oxygen. "How she responds in the next few hours will tell us more."

He guided Ron and me upstairs to a room in the intensive care unit. Laura, pale and motionless, was hooked up to a labyrinth of plastic tubes, pulsating machines, and blinking monitors. A ventilator did her breathing for her.

Her absence surrounded me.

An unsettling stillness replaced the chaotic rush of the day. Two nurses, one on each side of her bed, monitored Laura's vital signs while adjusting the tangle of tubes and wires around her. Neither said anything to us. Ron and I were left on our own to comprehend all Laura had been through, all she might have to yet face. We prayed.

It was nearing midnight. Ron drove home to pack some clothes for us and to check on Sara and Rachel. By the time he arrived at the house, they were already asleep. We'd decided to ask Margie to send them to school as usual until we knew more. Ron asked her to tell them, when they woke up, that Laura was recovering from a procedure. We didn't want Sara or Rachel worrying. We were the parents, we would do the worrying.

While Ron was gone, I turned to Laura's two nurses and, with a pleading pride, I told them that Laura loved school, was ranked sixth in her freshman class, and had a passion for writing and design. Part of me felt that if the nurses knew a little bit about her, they would take better care of her. They simply remained focused on her vital signs, and soon I stopped trying to engage them. At last, one nurse broke the silence by asking, "Would you like to talk to a social worker?" I nodded my head.

The social worker and I sat on folding chairs directly outside of Laura's room. He seemed shocked when I recounted the speed at which Laura's condition had deteriorated. "How can this have happened so out of the blue?" I asked. Like the chaplain, he listened without giving answers. When I told him we needed to tell friends and family about Laura's condition, he suggested we set up a CaringBridge webpage.

Later, I dozed on and off in the recliner in Laura's room. When Ron returned at about 3:00 a.m., I woke up and listened as he talked. He remained practical and calm, but he couldn't quite hide how worried he was. Without any more information about Laura's prognosis, we discussed "crisis mode" logistics, including outlining a plan to ensure that Sara and Rachel would be taken care of during the next few days. We then waited for the hours to pass, when we could again consult with the doctors.

The sun rose. Nothing changed. Ron's parents arrived from Evanston later in the morning; his sister Amy also joined us, after having driven four hours from Iowa's Quad Cities. Our rabbi arrived. His presence both comforted and alarmed me. He stood by Laura's bedside and chanted prayers in Hebrew that were frighteningly unfamiliar.

That afternoon, I created a CaringBridge account and wrote my first post with a bluntness that still stuns me, although I ended my words with a hopeful note: "Laura is fighting hard to get back to good health, and we want to send her as much love and encouragement from friends and family as possible."

My mom came to the hospital not long after and hugged me. She'd driven to Milwaukee as soon as she was able to find someone to take care of my dad, who had recently been diagnosed with multiple sclerosis (MS) and was now confined to a wheelchair. "We're going to fight hard for Laura," she declared.

"I think it's too late," I blurted out.

CHAPTER 3

Our Laura

When I think of myself, I think not only of a creative perfectionist, but as a girl with a willingness to help others and as someone who a friend can trust. Surely enough, I've learned that you just need to be yourself and show the world what you have to offer.

Laura Miller, "A Creative Perfectionist," 2006

Laura wasted little time. Right from the start, she filled her infant days with plenty of time observing her surroundings, mostly from the comfort of my arms. With a confidence and maturity far beyond her age, her brief babbling phase as a toddler quickly morphed into whole cohesive paragraphs, and she would chat eagerly with adults. These conversations expanded her knowledge and helped quench her nearly insatiable curiosity.

Even as a young child, Laura rarely played pretend, watched Disney movies, or played outside in the dirt. Instead, she created colorful "masterpieces" with neon-colored markers and glitter-glue, and she enjoyed making beaded necklaces. Once she was old enough to read, she relished playing games like Hangman, Boggle, and Monopoly. For Laura, fun meant some type of intellectual challenge. As early as second grade, she delighted in solving codes (and in creating her own), telling riddles, and trying to make up her own language. She wrote sentences backwards and then read them in the mirror, and she always got excited when she learned a new palindrome. She deciphered vanity license plates and found secret symbols within logos, such as the hidden arrow in the FedEx signage. As Laura grew older, she spent an inordinate amount of time drawing custom "signatures" in carefully selected colors and fonts for the "Lola" clothing line she dreamed of designing someday. She plastered the inside of her closet door with cutouts of inspiring quotes.

No matter her age, Laura always had a strong sense of herself beyond her years, and in many ways I thought of her as an old soul. In second grade, Laura wanted to fit in with the older kids, so she carried a copy of *Harry Potter* to school each day, even though she couldn't yet read the book by herself. In third grade, in order to convince us to buy her a pair of trendy eyeglasses, I believe she purposefully misidentified a few of the letters on her eye exam. By the fourth grade, she'd already begun sketching her own accessory line—purses, scarves, shoes, and earrings. In fifth grade, she began writing more and more stories and poems, both for school and on her own. It seemed to me that writing was Laura's way of figuring out who she was; it helped her explore life's big questions and search for the "rules" that might lessen the ambiguity of life.

Laura's creativity was so prolific that we have boxes of her designs and writings, all of which reflect her emotions, perspectives on life, and idiosyncrasies. In one of my favorite poems, she wrote:

> Getting dressed the next morning was quite easy to do,
> All I needed was to put on my clothes that were new.
> When I entered the school it seemed so strange,
> No one was laughing at me, for once; that was a change!
> Be yourself and show the world who you are,

Release your inner self, and learn to be your own superstar!
Now, I go to school and am not teased,
Luckily, my biggest fear has been eased!

Throughout elementary school, Laura preferred chatting at recess with the playground attendants rather than with children her own age. I believe this was how she dealt with her own shyness and her general uneasiness with unstructured free time. Yet, during the school day, she got along well with her classmates and often gravitated to those who—like herself—seemed in need of a friend. Laura would complain to me about teachers who played favorites or who didn't treat special needs students with enough respect; this became especially true after developing a close middle-school friendship with a girl who had Down's syndrome. Laura craved social acceptance just like any kid, but she also didn't want anyone, including herself, to feel excluded for any reason. If she believed a classmate's birthday might go unrecognized, she would take it upon herself to decorate that student's locker with wrapping paper, a handwritten birthday note, and a candy bar. She found happiness in her classmates' surprise and appreciation.

Much of Laura's self-esteem came from pleasing her teachers, a trait—in addition to perfectionism—that she seemed to have inherited from me. When Laura filled in school worksheets with her meticulous handwriting, she would often use all the white space on the page. She would write vertically along the margins if she needed to, and she would often put an arrow at the bottom to indicate that she'd continued writing on the reverse side. She earned good grades not just for my approval or her teachers' recognition, but because she demanded a high level of achievement for herself—she called herself a "creative perfectionist" and tried to exceed expectations in whatever she did. She often became anxious prior to exams, and she would get frustrated when she didn't receive an *A* on a test, but she was wise enough to understand, at least philosophically, that grades weren't the ultimate goal of learning. In her own words, Laura once said in an essay: "The grade or score you get isn't the most important part of the learning experience. The knowledge is what gets you places."

During the summers before sixth through ninth grades, Laura opted to attend a three-week academic program at Northwestern University rather than going to a more traditional summer camp with Sara. We accepted her decision, especially given that Laura hated skinned knees, sweating, and bugs. For Laura, swimming, riding bikes, and enjoying lazy summer days offered little appeal—living in a college dorm, studying high-school-level material, and socializing with academically minded teens was far more intriguing. These advanced classes allowed her to examine the world in a more in-depth way and helped her figure out the type of person she wanted to be. In her social justice course, when she was just twelve years old, she wrote:

> Even though I think of myself now as a tolerant person, I would like to be more accepting of people's differences and accept people for who they really are. I also want to appreciate what I have, and all of the privileges that we Americans don't think of on a daily basis. I really want to have a full understanding of what it means to have running water, religious freedom, a civil government, and such.

Laura's academic focus, however, didn't overshadow her love for all things fashion. As a young child, she would rummage through her dresser several times each day to find the right outfit for the "occasion." As she got older, she progressed to carefully selecting ensembles for her Barbie dolls, and by middle school was already using a sewing machine and had started devising her own simple clothing patterns. She would spend hours in her bedroom sketching designs, explicitly noting the patterns, colors, and fabric types she planned to use for each outfit. Her "Lola" fashion line included categories such as flowy/bohemian, the Elizabethan Era, and African-tribal-inspired wear. Yet, although Laura's designs were sophisticated for her age, she gave childlike names to her creations—her "Lolashirts collection" had names like Cupcake, Whipped Cream, and Popsicle.

Laura's love of fashion extended to interior design as she got older. One of my favorite drawings is of her dream house, a circular home with an all-glass exterior. Her ideas blended sophisticated style with youthful flair—she detailed adult elements like elaborate candleholders and a black-granite backsplash for the stove, but she also drew a fish-tank floor in the living room and specified white, fluffy carpeting for the laundry room.

Laura's fascination with style puzzled Ron and me because her interest certainly didn't come from either of us. She coveted designer brands and followed the latest celebrity styles, while I was oblivious to fashion trends and overpriced labels. Yet, one critical glance from her about my outfit would convince me to return to my closet and rethink my choice. When we watched award shows, Laura would comment on each red-carpet outfit, while I would do my best at feigning interest. My routine for getting ready in the morning was quick and practical; Laura would wake up early to straighten her hair before each school day, after having already agonized over her outfit the night before.

Laura had high standards for the way she presented herself to the world, but not in a superficial way—her style, I believe, stemmed more from her sense of individuality. Fashion gave her a way to express herself while also bonding with her friends through popular culture. Yet Laura wasn't naive about the fashion industry's unrealistic beauty standards and wrote passionately about how it shouldn't promote an unhealthy lifestyle. One of her goals was to "flip the world of fashion upside down" and make the industry a more inclusive place for everyone, no matter their body type:

> With millions of teenagers thinking that beauty is limited, feelings need to be changed shortly, or else the world will have to cope with a generation that cannot learn to accept themselves as they are. Having a positive attitude toward fashion and appearance needs to be stressed to young adults or else [...] little things like a birthmark or a pointy chin will be maximized into bigger issues. Models may have looks that are coveted by others, but making sure that the attitudes and outlooks of the majority of the population stay positive should definitely be a top priority. If extremely skinny models keep making their way down the runway, the world of fashion will eventually need to answer the question of defining skinny from reality.

Laura's preoccupation with her style could occasionally make her stubborn, and that stubbornness meant she sometimes needed my help. For her freshman homecoming dance, Laura was dead set on a "sophisticated" strapless-dress-look, even though I'd cautioned that a strapless dress probably wouldn't work on her slender body. She chose not to take my advice. An hour before the pre-dance dinner, she ran into my bedroom in tears—each time she raised her arms, the dress slipped several inches down her not-yet-matured frame. I'm still impressed with myself for improvising a solution so quickly: I dug out an old formal handbag from my closet and cut off its long, black cord. I repurposed the cord into two straps for the dress, which I then draped over Laura's shoulders and secured as discreetly as I could with safety pins. Laura hugged me, wiped away her tears, and then hurried back to her room to finish getting ready. A little while later, I watched happily (and with relief) as she climbed into the car with her friends.

Although motivated and self-sufficient, Laura needed me as her anchor—a role I enjoyed, but one which required balancing her needs with those of her sisters. This was no easy task as Laura relished being the center of attention. She almost always completed her homework at the kitchen table, in the middle of the family action, rather than at her desk in her room. She multi-tasked as she worked, simultaneously asking Ron about his recent business deals and/or inquiring about who would be at my next NCJW or MJF meeting.

Even though her blue eyes and slight build more closely resembled Ron's side of the family, Laura's psyche and mine were deeply linked in a way that's hard to describe. Each afternoon, from the time I picked her up from school until about 7:00 p.m., I could sense her angst as she processed her day. She shared a lot of her inner thoughts with me, but often only on her own schedule, such as late on Sunday nights when she started worrying about the week ahead. Sitting on the edge of her bed, I'd muster my patience, talk through her apprehensions, and brainstorm solutions with her. Laura would often disagree with the answers I offered, but underneath her objections I knew she appreciated our discussions. She told me many times that I was her best friend—and I felt like she was mine, too.

Laura wanted to please me, but that didn't mean she wouldn't tune out my "nagging mom" requests to clean up her bedroom or put away her art supplies. I can count on two hands, though, the number of time-outs I had to give her; talking things out, even when we frustrated each other, proved more effective. Although I was her mom, we often interacted as intellectual equals, and we were almost always able to come to a compromise or mutual understanding.

Laura was well suited for the firstborn-child role and liked being the oldest, and this became especially evident after Rachel came along. When Rachel was a baby, Laura enjoyed making her sister smile; as Rachel became older, Laura would construct and decorate paper houses with her, and then ask Ron to judge which was "the best." Laura and Sara were on more equal footing. Although they competed with each other at times and fought for Rachel's finicky allegiance, they got along well and would often play dress-up in our finished basement with the costumes we'd accumulated over the years. I also remember many times when all three girls spontaneously began dancing and singing, with over-exaggerated movements, to their favorite songs from *Wicked*. As the oldest, Laura wanted to set a good example for her siblings and would become frustrated with herself when she failed to live up to her own standards. "From experience with younger siblings," she once wrote, "I know that almost everything that I do, my sisters want to try . . . and then the ripple effect will evolve from that."

In contrast to her apparent maturity and drive, Laura was surprisingly willing to suspend reality when it might benefit her. Up until the start of middle school, she wrote more than a few notes to the tooth fairy and placed them under her pillow. She often included both her email and home addresses to ensure a response.

Dear Tooth Fairy,

I swallowed my tooth and I had a big fit that it happened, so my mom said I could write you a letter, so here it is! First, can you be my pen pal? We would write every night and I would put it under my pillow so you can pick it up. Second, you know the aliens that are found in prize machines? You have to pay 25 cents to get one. But my parents wouldn't let me, so I thought that you might want to give me 100 small aliens. If you can't put all of them under my pillow, put them under my bed. And I'll pick them up in the morning. Third, if you can't do this, then I won't have a fit and I won't be mad. Anyways, who are you? Please be positive. Write back tonight.

Laura Miller

P.S. My sister is Sara Miller. She is six and lost six teeth (I think). My other sister is Rachel Miller. She is three and hasn't lost any teeth but is really cute and under her pillow can you put some aliens also?

And by the way, give Sara a Dell laptop. Also, can you also get me (Laura) a Dell laptop? Thanks!

Also in contrast to Laura's maturity were her fears. She played it safe and tried to steer clear of blood, germs, the blaring of smoke alarms, and the beeping of carbon monoxide detectors. She never completely lost her aversion to the dark, strangers, or being alone, although I didn't realize just how extreme her phobias were until one afternoon when I ran a few quick errands without her. Laura was eleven at the time, and I was sure she was ready to stay alone for a half-hour. Regrettably, while I was out, the meter-reader from the electric company entered our yard. Laura said he wasn't in uniform, and I believe that's what scared her the most. The man didn't come into the house, but she was so traumatized that she later wrote about it in a school essay. I felt guilty; Laura's maturity had given me more confidence in her than she had in herself. When we talked about her essay, I specifically remember her telling me about the security precautions she planned to take as an adult: a burglar alarm, always-locked doors, and perhaps a big dog.

Laura's confidence increased, and her general anxiety decreased, around the time she joined BBYO. She loved participating in their social and community service events, and she liked connecting with other Jewish teens from across the nearby suburbs. I can still picture her smile when, just after being inducted, we ran into several of her BBYO friends. They greeted her with big hugs and plenty of giggles.

Laura's Jewish identity and spirituality were also strengthened during our family's trip to Israel over winter break of her freshman year. For ten days, we'd toured religious sites and learned about Israel's biblical and secular history. Laura developed an emotional connection to the country, but the trip also expanded her political perspectives and views on religious diversity. In an English assignment, completed only days after we returned from the trip, she wrote:

> I now know that religion is simply a way of living your life. Just because somebody chooses to live their life differently than I do doesn't mean that I should look down upon

them. It means that I should look at them and be inspired to learn more about their faith, more about what they believe.

Just before we left Israel, we visited the oldest section of Israel's Western Wall, a sacred relic from the era of the Second Temple. Observing a long-standing tradition, Laura scribbled her hopes and wishes on a piece of paper and inserted it into a crevice between the stones. I'll never know what that paper said, exactly, but I believe she wished—as I did—for continued health and happiness for our family and friends.

CHAPTER 4

As the World Dulled

Third Week of February 2009

We spent the rest of Thursday waiting by Laura's bedside. Waiting on news from the doctors, waiting for Laura to wake up, waiting for anything that could give us hope. The ventilator pushed air into her lungs, machines beeped, nurses hovered by her side. Yet nothing changed.

The surgery to remove Laura's tumor, initially scheduled for Friday, had been postponed due to her lack of responsiveness. The doctors needed to see significant improvement before they could operate. And so, we waited. We prayed for the doctors to do their best, prayed for Laura's eyes to open, prayed for normalcy to return to our family, prayed to wake from our nightmare.

Because events happened so fast, Ron and I hadn't been able to establish a strong relationship with any one doctor, so we appreciated it when Laura's pediatrician introduced us to Dr. M., her colleague and a pediatric oncologist. Dr. M. generously acted as our go-between and helped us interpret the onslaught of medical terms. He suspected Laura's critical condition was caused by a lack of oxygen from the night before; yesterday afternoon's MRI findings did not indicate the extent of the damage.

That evening, our extended family members left and went to our home to stay with Sara and Rachel. My mother remained at

Laura's bedside. A nurse handed Ron the key to a room one floor below, where we could spend the night and try to get a few hours of rest. We were both exhausted, but I wondered how anyone could expect us to sleep.

Ron opened the door to the windowless, closet-like room. Unable to locate the light switch, we fumbled our way to the narrow beds, one against each wall, spaced only two feet apart. In the dark, we lay down and did our best to talk things through, despite our fear and disorientation. We worried that Laura had suffered brain damage, that she'd be in a coma-like state forever. Our seemingly controlled and predictable life had—literally overnight—become cruelly warped; our family's future had suddenly been upended and now bore little resemblance to the hopes and dreams we'd held only one day ago.

We wondered how to best share what was happening with Sara and Rachel—what to tell them, how much to tell them, when to tell them. We agreed they should be kept to their routines until we knew more. If we brought them to the hospital, they would sense our dread and have questions that we couldn't answer. We couldn't cope with their fears on top of our own—we had to focus our energy exclusively on Laura. For the first time, as parents, we would have to trust our family and community to take care of our children when we could not.

After ten minutes, I abruptly sat up and told Ron I was going back upstairs. If Laura woke up, I wanted to be the first person she saw. I wanted to explain everything we knew in a way that wouldn't frighten her. But she didn't move all night, not even a little bit.

Early the next morning, after my mom went home to Evanston, a nurse handed me Laura's three stud earrings in a small plastic bag. For months, Laura had pleaded with me for permission to get a third piercing in her right ear. Why had I waited so long to consent to her simple request? How could I ever have thought a tiny pinprick in her earlobe was important in the grand scheme of things?

As I stood by her bedside, an unnatural stillness again enveloped me. "Laura, when you get better," I said with a falsely upbeat voice, "how about we go shopping and find you the perfect pair of jeans? Or we could go to the Apple Store. I'd love to do that with you." Laura's eyelids fluttered. My heart pounded with unexpected hope as the monitors' alarms beeped. Had my daughter responded to my voice?

"She has to be kept calm!" a nurse snapped. She motioned for me to be quiet and to move away from the bed. Even still, I left the room elated; I headed to the overnight room to share the news with Ron. Maybe Laura was getting better. Maybe she would wake up soon.

By Thursday night, Sara and Rachel knew that their sister's illness was serious, and news of Laura's condition had spread through both her high school and our community. A few friends came to the hospital to support us, and by Friday we were flooded with generous offers of help: one friend said she would drive Sara and Rachel wherever they needed to go; another proposed that they spend the night at her home. Others simply asked how they could help. We didn't know what to say. Each offer was comforting, but what we needed, our friends couldn't give us.

Friday marked our third day in the hospital. Laura still showed no improvement. Dr. M. said that another MRI was scheduled for the next day. "That should tell us why her condition is clinically worse than the scans have indicated so far."

That afternoon, I watched as two nurses lifted Laura's legs

and encased them, one after the other, in plastic-like sleeves; a machine then pumped air into each. When I asked what the device was for, one of the nurses explained, "These sleeves will massage her legs so her muscles don't atrophy." Alarm shot through me: if Laura's muscles needed such basic stimulation, her condition was surely more severe than I'd been allowing myself to believe.

I paused outside of Laura's room, trying to collect myself as my heart pounded and started to burn. I told a nurse about the pain. "This is a pediatric hospital," she said firmly and with a surprising lack of empathy. "You'll have to go to the emergency room at the general hospital across the street if you need to get checked out." My body was beginning to suffer from constant worry and lack of sleep, but I certainly wasn't going to leave my daughter. With urging from a friend who'd recently arrived, I returned to the waiting room to lie down on a couch until the pressure in my chest subsided.

Later that afternoon, we called Sara and told her we needed to cancel her *bat mitzvah* (scheduled for the following weekend). Sara agreed it was the right thing to do; she was far more concerned with Laura's health than any religious ceremony, even one that she'd been anticipating for so many years. Ron called our event coordinator and asked her to inform the caterer and DJ. Then, with a determined efficiency I'm still thankful for, Ron divided up—between Margie, my brother, and our parents—the list of family and friends who needed to be called. Even in the midst of our shock, we understood that our guests needed time to cancel their travel plans, including their flights and hotel reservations. According to Ron, everyone was shocked and concerned, and many assured him they would be there for Sara when her special day did arrive.

Friday evening, two friends delivered a home-cooked *Shabbat* meal to the hospital. I had no appetite, but Ron pleaded with me to eat a few bites. That same night, Margie brought a bag full of get-well notes from Laura's classmates so we could read them to her when she woke up. As I scanned through their notes and cards, I knew her friends' kind words and genuine concern would make Laura smile.

"We all miss you at school, and today was a really weird, upsetting, shocking experience for all of us."

"You are one of the nicest girls I've ever met and I'm praying for you every day. Feel better soon!"

"You mean more to the school and to your peers than you may think."

"Through the tears we all know how strong and smart you are and are hoping for you to make it through. Today is Friday and normally people are happy, almost bouncing off the walls. Today's nothing like that. Everyone seemed to be in a daze, even those who didn't know you. Just two days ago, you were solving math problems and asking the most insightful questions about persuasive essays."

Sara, too, had written several letters. Although only twelve-and-a-half years old, she understood the seriousness of Laura's illness, even if she didn't know all the details.

"Laura, you are so amazing. I know that you are as bright as this piece of paper. Actually, you are brighter. I hope you feel even better, and when you're feeling better, you will even be brighter. I love you more than you could ever imagine! XOXO, Sara"

"Dear Laura, I hope you feel better. You are so much fun and I hate seeing you sick. I want your headaches to go away and you to be happy again. You're the best sister and a good role model. I love you so much! Sara"

"Laura, I'm sending you lots of love! I hope it arrives soon and safely. I can't stop thinking about you because you are just so amazing. I can't say how much in words I want you to get well! You are so awesome and fabulous! Sara"

Later that night, exhausted and drained, Ron and I asked Dr. M. if we should go home to get some sleep, then return in the morning before the MRI. "I wouldn't recommend it," he replied. "From my experience, families will go over the events in the hospital for the rest of their lives." We took his advice and spent the overnight hours rotating once again between Laura's bed and the small overnight room. To this day, I remain thankful that we stayed.

On Saturday morning, we watched as five nurses and orderlies disentangled the maze of tubes and wires that were attached to our daughter. We followed as she was wheeled to the MRI suite, then Ron and I went into the waiting room, the same room in which I had waited three days earlier—a lifetime ago.

The pediatric neurosurgeon entered the waiting room and looked directly at us. "Laura has suffered a massive brain bleed," he informed us in a steady, subdued tone. "An infarct resulting from the increased intracranial pressure. It's catastrophic and irreversible."

The world dulled.

We listened as the neurosurgeon gave more specifics and confirmed what we already knew in our hearts: Laura was dead. Machines were now keeping our precious daughter breathing, but she was not alive.

No bells tolled. No somber music played. No tears yet flowed. Ron and I held each other up as we staggered in a stupor toward the elevator. Fourteen years. That was all the time we would have with our Laura.

Upstairs, in a private waiting room, we delivered the devastating news to our family. I don't remember much about their reactions; I've blocked those memories out. I remember the room itself, though—two upholstered armchairs, a wooden coffee table, a corner lamp, and boxes of tissues that would soon be empty. I found myself focused on a folded blanket on the sofa—a handmade quilt, sewn by volunteers, intended to offer comfort. But rather than provide comfort, it confirmed the awful truth we'd just learned. The awful, unfathomable truth.

Ron and I had believed keeping Sara and Rachel away from the hospital was the best choice we could make for their well-being, but now we knew they needed the chance to say goodbye to their older sister. We still didn't know what—or how—to tell them, though. We could barely take in the reality ourselves.

Through a raging snowstorm, Margie and her husband Jon drove Sara and Rachel to the hospital. Margie later told me she was relentlessly questioned by the girls during the entire half-hour drive. With a composure and skill that still awes me, she answered their questions without revealing too much. It was our job, as parents, to talk to Sara and Rachel, and Margie respected our wishes. She was so protective of our daughters that, when she'd received my heartbreaking phone call, Margie had first moved out of the girls' earshot, and then, a few minutes later, she called her landline (from her cell phone) and pretended to have a short, composed conversation with me. I'll forever be indebted to her for her grace under pressure.

They all arrived at the hospital around noon. I barely remember how or what Ron and I told Sara and Rachel, and I remember even less about their reactions. My brain has blocked it all out, which is probably for the best. Even now, almost ten years later, I recall some moments with intensity and others not at all. I do remember that Sara and Rachel wanted to see Laura. I do remember the social worker explaining to them what Laura would look like attached to all the machines. I do remember her giving both of them remembrance journals to record their emotions. And I especially remember cringing when Sara and Rachel returned to the waiting room and showed me their reddish-stained hands; the social worker had painted the palms of all three sisters to create a handprint-collage, and I remember being upset that their hands—especially Laura's—had been painted without my permission. Today the collage remains buried in a memory box.

Sara and Rachel had barely finished showing me their hands when a woman wearing a white lab coat approached us. She was in her early thirties, and her tone was warm as she introduced herself. "I'm Emily from the Wisconsin Donor Network," she said. "I'm so sorry for your loss." Her expression of sympathy was the first time we'd heard these specific words of condolence. I stiffened, shocked at their meaning. How could her sentiment—however sincere—possibly be directed at us? Neither Ron nor

I responded, but she continued. "I'm here to ask if you would consider donating Laura's organs," she said gently.

She repeated what the doctors had told us: Laura's brain stem was no longer functioning, meaning that she was legally dead. Then she explained how Laura's organs could save as many as eight lives and improve the quality of life for as many as fifty other people.[1] These conversations were probably routine for Donor Network employees, but my stomach lurched. I listened in a daze as she concluded, "I'll come back in a little while to answer any questions. The decision is completely up to you."

Our agonizing reality now became all the more surreal. That we—only hours after learning of Laura's irreversible brain damage—could be considering removing her generous heart, her healthy lungs, or her beautiful blue eyes, was beyond comprehension. Laura had been healthy and in school not even four days earlier. She should've been preparing to present her science and history fair projects alongside her classmates. She should've been sketching dress designs and hanging out with her sisters and friends. She should not be here. This was not how her life was supposed to be. This was not how *our* lives were supposed to be.

Ron and I always believed organ donation to be a noble and generous concept, but we'd never once imagined having to make this heart-wrenching choice for our daughter. We'd discussed many ethical issues with Laura, but not this one; now, as her parents, the decision was ours to make. A decision we didn't know *how* to make.

We looked across the room at our rabbi. "Judaism views saving a life to be the holiest of *mitzvahs*—not only encouraged but mandated," he said in a definitive yet compassionate voice. He

---

1. See < https://share.upmc.com/2015/04/the-impact-of-one-organ-donor> for more information.

counseled us, saying that according to the Talmud, saving one life is tantamount to saving the world. If Laura's organs could save someone, donation was the decision the Jewish tradition would encourage and even sanctify.

Ron and I liked the idea of Laura helping to save another person's life, but we had wanted a miracle to save hers—and part of me was still hoping for that miracle. I thought about what I believed happened after death. On the one hand, I'd been taught that we're born, then we die—from dust to dust. If that were true, Laura's organs would do nothing more than decompose uselessly in the ground. Yet, I'd also been taught that when the Messiah comes, the dead will be brought back to life. If that were true, would the dead need their bodies to be intact for resurrection? Would Laura—under any circumstance—need her organs in some way in the afterlife? What happens to us after death now became a very practical question—a question I didn't have an answer to.

By now, it was the middle of the afternoon, five hours after the final MRI: it felt like days had passed. Sara and Rachel listened to our conversation as we debated. Then Sara spoke up with a confidence that still surprises Ron and me to this day. "How can you say 'no' if we can help save someone's life?" she asked. "You *have* to donate her organs."

This grief wasn't ours only. Sara and Rachel had lost their older sister: they deserved a voice. Ron and I had only one chance to make the right decision—if we disagreed with them, they might never forgive us. I turned to Rachel. She nodded her head in bewildered agreement with Sara. Ron ran his fingers through his hair, composing himself. We looked at each other, silent and stunned, and then agreed to the unfathomable.

We told Emily our decision when she returned a little while

later. Her shoulders relaxed as she began discussing with us which organs we would authorize for donation. Ron and I didn't know what to do. Emily once again left the room to give us time to think. I glanced at the disturbingly detailed list of body parts and froze. Nothing in my life had prepared me for this.

Ron focused painstakingly on the list. We soon agreed to donate Laura's internal organs—heart, both lungs, both kidneys, liver, and pancreas—but we decided not to donate her corneas. At the time, we believed her entire eyeballs would be transplanted, and neither of us could bear the thought of seeing Laura's eyes in someone else. We later learned that only the lenses are removed for cornea donations. In hindsight, I wish we had donated them.

We each signed the paperwork, and we each voiced our consent. With that done, Ron took Sara and Rachel into Laura's room for a final goodbye. I stayed in the waiting room, still numb from our decision. They didn't stay long, but Sara later told me that seconds after she'd left Laura's room, she went back to say, "I love you." She wanted those to be the last words Laura heard from her.

My brother Steven took Sara and Rachel home—he later told us that because we'd entrusted him with our two surviving daughters, he'd never driven more carefully in his life. He remembers that the girls were unusually quiet during the drive. They hardly spoke at all, apart from asking when Ron and I would be coming home.

Doctors and nurses streamed in and out of the waiting room over the next two hours. We asked Emily what was happening. "Cancerous cells might have spread from Laura's tumor," she replied. "The doctors are trying to figure out if her organs are viable." She told us that insertion of the shunt might have broken Laura's blood-brain barrier and caused malignant cells to enter her bloodstream. We waited as the doctors, in another room, conferred. We wondered why they hadn't assessed these risks before asking us, on the worst day of our lives, to make such a grueling decision.

In the Jewish tradition, the dead are buried as soon as possible, often within twenty-four hours. Once Laura's organs were deemed viable, we told Emily we wanted the funeral to be on Monday morning. The organ donation team, the medical staff, and the funeral home would have to work together quickly to honor our wishes. Emily made that happen. We learned that a match for Laura's liver had already been found. A surgical team would recover Laura's organs in the early morning hours.

Now, there was nothing left to do. There were no more forms to sign, decisions to make, or doctors to talk to. Knowing it was now our turn to say goodbye, Ron and I followed the social worker down the hallway to Laura's room.

My brain disconnected from my body.

The room was quieter than before. The lights were dimmed, the machines whirred more softly, and the monitors were now darkened. Ron stepped forward and kissed Laura on the forehead. I held Laura's limp hand and gazed at her expressionless face. My mind numbed. Finally, with a hoarse voice, I uttered, "I love you," before I tore myself away and left the room. I had said goodbye to Laura—and to a part of myself as well.

Ron stayed for a few more moments before joining me. Neither of us knew what to do. How were we supposed to know what to do?

I hugged the quilted grief blanket as Ron and I walked down the long hospital hallway to the parking garage. I blinked as the frigid wind stung my eyes.

CHAPTER 5

Lost in the Desert

Last Week of February 2009

Widow is the word for a woman who's lost her husband, *orphan* is the term for someone whose parents are both deceased. There's no name, however, for a mother and father who lose a child. Yet, as our rabbi drove us home from the hospital, that's what I realized Ron and I now were: parents whose firstborn had been ripped from our lives.

Once home, we managed to say a quick hello to the few close family members who were staying at our house, then hurried to find Sara and Rachel. They were in the living room huddled in front of the computer, where they were taking comfort in the stream of get-well wishes on Laura's Facebook page and on her CaringBridge page. I was thankful they had something to focus on as Ron and I sat down with them and began reading the messages. Every time we scrolled down the screen, more hopeful, supportive comments appeared. Laura would've been overwhelmed to learn how much she meant to her friends and classmates. We read every comment but didn't respond to any; there was nothing to say.

Ron and I knew we had to announce Laura's death, especially as her funeral would be in just two days. Crafting our sentences as carefully as we could, we wrote an email, although the words didn't seem real even as we typed them. When we finished, Ron's finger hovered over the keyboard. We looked at each other in disbelief. At 9:12 p.m., he pressed send.

> With tremendous sorrow, we need to tell you that our beautiful daughter Laura died this evening. The funeral will be held on either Monday or Tuesday at Congregation Shalom. We're certain she heard all your prayers, and all your good wishes mean so much to us. For the time being, please continue to communicate with us only through email.
>
> — Susan, Ron, Sara, and Rachel

Within seconds, shocked condolences flooded the screen, replacing the hopeful get-well posts. Messages from close friends, family, and acquaintances alike expressed a shared grief. We were alone in our house, yet we felt embraced by our community.

Ron and I tucked Sara and Rachel in their beds and hoped they would be able to sleep. Laura's room, of course, remained empty and dark. As we passed it, for an instant, "Where's Laura?" popped into my head, almost as if my brain had suppressed the nightmare of the past four days. Now that we were back in our own home, I wanted a simple answer to my question. Where was Laura? Where was she?

I sighed heavily as reality hit me. We headed to our bedroom, down the same hallway where Laura had collapsed, the same hallway where the paramedics had rushed in to treat her. Four days ago, when the rules we'd observed so conscientiously had betrayed us.

I crawled under the covers, the clothes I'd worn in the hospital crumpled in a pile next to my bed. I stared at the ceiling, unable to take in the flood of spinning sensations, as if I were plastered against the wall of a rotating, gravity-defying amusement park ride. The floor, the foundation of my life, had fallen away, and it seemed nothing was holding me together except the spinning itself.

Still stunned, Ron and I talked briefly about the preparations we would need to make the next day. The idea of planning Laura's funeral overwhelmed us. Ron soon rolled onto his stomach, buried his face in his pillow, and pulled the covers around his face. I lay back, but my mind continued to whirl: How could Laura have attended school on Tuesday and stopped breathing on Wednesday? How could something as common as teenage headaches be a deadly cancer? How had four days, days that I still couldn't process as real, torn apart our family?

As I lay in the dark, I worried about having enough energy to be able to comfort Sara and Rachel in the midst of my own grief. They would need Ron and me like never before in the coming days. All I could focus on was keeping them safe, on protecting them in a way that I'd be unable to do for Laura.

I willed myself to sleep.

The next morning, on Sunday, Ron and my brother went to select a gravesite. Two Jewish cemeteries on the other side of town had been recommended to us, but I didn't want to visit either of them—I trusted Ron to make the decision. Instead, I stayed at home and talked with the family and friends who were filling the house with their presence and support. In the afternoon, my mother-in-law suggested I go upstairs and take a nap. I'd barely slept since Tuesday night, yet I didn't want to be by myself. Talking made me feel weirdly empowered and in control of our story—in control of *something*. Talking distracted me from the cruel reality that my brain was only now beginning to accept.

Ron called me from the cemetery's office. "We found a

gravesite away from the road in a wooded area. It's near some other younger people's graves." His description reminded me of a real estate listing rather than a final resting place for Laura. "I'm going to buy plots for both of us, right beside hers," he continued. "Is that okay?"

A cold wave of realization swept through me, and I paused as my own mortality confronted me. "I guess you're right," I replied. "We can't leave her alone. Just do whatever you think we should do." Ron later told me that the cemetery caretaker had then spread out his tattered property map, located the plots, and, with a pencil, written down all three of us among other smudged names and half-erased marks.

That afternoon we visited the funeral home. The office was a nondescript storefront less than ten minutes from our house—we'd passed it countless times yet never had a reason to notice it. Now, as Ron and I entered, a man in a black suit welcomed us. He introduced us to the funeral director, who was seated behind a desk. He expressed his sympathy, then turned toward his computer. "We shouldn't be here," I thought. "Why are we here?"

The director bombarded us with questions as he filled in the obituary form: cause of death; surviving relatives; dates and times for the funeral, burial, and *shiva*. When he asked where we would like contributions to be made in Laura's memory, I remembered my mother's advice from earlier in the day. She'd suggested that we direct donations to a single memorial fund so we'd be able to channel the monies to charities that were most meaningful to our family. Ron and I knew someone at the Jewish Community Foundation and believed she could take care of all the financial details easily; Ron gave the director her name.

The director led us to a windowless room, lined floor-to-ceiling with caskets: simple pine boxes, elaborately carved oak coffins—models in wood, copper, and bronze, each available in varying sizes. Which one did we want? Ron shook his head: we were being asked to survey the options as if we were choosing a coffee table rather than selecting our daughter's coffin. We decided on a modern casket with simple lines; it was in a style similar to the IKEA bedroom set Laura had picked out for herself only two or three years earlier. I hoped she would have approved of our choice.

As the director was seeing us out, he mentioned, in a casual way, that since it was already Sunday afternoon, Laura's obituary wouldn't be printed until tomorrow—the same day of the funeral and burial. I stopped walking and gasped. "But by then the funeral will already be over!" I cried. "How will people know about the services?"

"Don't worry. They'll know," he said with confidence. "Anybody who needs to be there will be." I accepted his answer as we practically fled from the funeral home.

Our rabbi came to our house after dinner that evening. As he removed his hat and coat, I thought about the many congregants he had consoled over the years. I wondered, though, how often he'd prepared a eulogy for a fourteen-year-old.

Even though he'd met Laura many times, he asked us to tell him about her in our own words. How were we supposed to describe all that was Laura in a few sentences? Even if we talked for an eternity, we would never come close to capturing her spirit, her kindness, her ambition, her creativity, her love for life. We shared a few descriptions and anecdotes, hoping to convey some sense of our beautiful daughter and our relationship with her.

Our rabbi left our house forty-five minutes later. He'd listened attentively, but he hadn't taken any notes. Ron and I worried that he might make mistakes about the details of Laura's life or, more significantly, fail to convey her essence in his eulogy. One more worry in the flood of uncertainties and fears that were now threatening to drown us.

An hour later, the funeral home's driver called to ask us what we wanted to eat on the ride between the funeral and the burial. Did we want turkey, tuna fish, or cheese sandwiches; mustard or mayo; chips or fruit? The mundane intermingled with the maudlin.

Dressing myself on the day of my daughter's funeral struck me as unusually cruel. I grabbed my black pantsuit from the closet, then pulled on my tall dress boots slowly. In the bathroom, I fumbled through my cosmetics. I wanted to look presentable but debated if applying makeup would seem disrespectful. I left the mascara on the counter but shoved a lipstick and blush into my purse.

Sara and Rachel shouted that the limousine had pulled into our driveway. We piled in. Sara held Ron's hand as she stared out the window, and Rachel buried her head in my lap. After being driven the three miles to our synagogue, we were guided to a classroom where our extended families had gathered.

The funeral director pinned a two-inch black ribbon onto the left side of my jacket, close to my heart. Our rabbi then recited a prayer as he tore my ribbon—symbolizing how death tears apart the fabric of life. The *kriah* ribbons were also pinned—and then torn—for Ron, Sara, and Rachel as well. By tradition, our torn *kriah* were supposed to be worn each day during the *shiva* mourning period. Ron and I wore our ribbons the first day, but we chose not to re-pin them to our outfits later on.

We would also choose not to attend the customary daily

minyan services during the thirty-day *sheloshim* period. Focusing our attention on Sara and Rachel was far more important. For the sake of our daughters and ourselves, we needed to regain some sense of stability and normalcy. We didn't believe daily mourning rituals would help us achieve that, even if tradition told us otherwise.

We had no idea how many people would come to pay their respects that morning, but as our rabbi and cantor guided us into the sanctuary, we saw that our synagogue was overflowing with people, with many standing in the back. We were stunned; over twelve-hundred guests had come to offer their condolences, had rearranged their Monday morning on less than two days' notice to mourn Laura.

An eerie and reverential silence followed us as we walked toward our seats in the first row. Sara sat to my left; Rachel, sandwiched in between Ron and me, sat on my right. They were too young to face such a heartbreaking loss. We had done our best as parents to shield them from life's normal hardships, never foreseeing an event like this. How could we help them through their grief and shelter them from future tragedies? How would we be able to keep them safe when we'd been so powerless to protect Laura?

Two years earlier, in this beautiful sanctuary, Laura had read from the Torah at her *bat mitzvah* and had been welcomed as a young adult into the Jewish community. Now her short life was over. Not only would she never reach legal adulthood, but she would also never experience the joys of being an independent woman, a wife, or a mother. So much promise, gone.

Rabbi Barbara, who'd officiated at Laura's baby-naming ceremony, began the service by talking about her close relationship with our family and her memories of Laura as a young child. I heard her words without wanting to listen to their meaning.

When our rabbi made his way to the pulpit, I held my breath. "Children aren't supposed to die before their parents," he began. Silence filled the sanctuary. "In fourteen years," he continued, "Laura did more than most people achieve in a lifetime." My heart expanded with pride as he described Laura's ever-present smile and praised her for wanting to make the world a better place. His eulogy captured Laura as wholly as any speech can summarize a person's existence.

At the end of our rabbi's remarks, I lowered my eyes again as he read a few words that Ron and I composed the night before but had decided against delivering ourselves:

> From the moment Laura was born, she was a very special child. She loved life. She had a thirst for knowledge, friendship, and justice. She loved helping others, and she had a true sense of purpose. She was a beacon of sunshine, and she was a role model for us and everyone she touched. Laura was wise beyond her years. She told her sisters and us every day that she loved us. And we told her that we loved her.

> The outpouring of love has been overwhelming and will help us get through this very difficult time. The letters, postings, and support are unbelievable. We will cherish these thoughts and memories of Laura forever.

> Laura lived each day to the fullest. She will live on in our hearts and minds forever. We feel very blessed to have been her parents and thank each and every one of you for your love, friendship, support, and prayers.

When I glanced up, Laura's *tallit*-draped casket was ten feet in front of me. I didn't know if it had been there for the whole service, or if it had somehow been brought forward without my noticing. How could Laura be so close and yet so far away at the same time?

The service concluded with more prayers, recited in both Hebrew and English. We then followed the casket, which was ushered by our closest male friends and relatives, down the aisle. As we followed, I was struck by the number of people who surrounded us. I felt the embrace of our community with an intensity that still overpowers me today.

The burial was private. At the cemetery, about thirty minutes away, the driver opened the door for me. My teeth chattered in the twenty-degree February afternoon as Rachel and I walked up the small hill, stepping on the icy grass in between the head-stones. Ron walked ahead of me with Sara, and his parents, at his side.

As the ceremony began, I thought about the funerals for my grandmother and my great-aunt Hannah, who had both lived until their mid-nineties. During their services, I stood toward the back of the crowd and wiped my tears away discreetly. Now there was no hiding: Ron, Sara, Rachel, and I stood in the front row. My eyes remained dry—this couldn't be real, so how could I cry? When we began chanting the *Kaddish*, a prayer for the dead which ironically lacks any mention of death, my throat tightened; I was only able to utter every other word.

With the prayers over and the casket lowered, a backhoe brought the cement vault cover, which dangled from a heavy steel chain, to the grave. As the backhoe arrived at the open plot, its heavy wheels lost traction in the newly unearthed mud. As if in slow motion, the backhoe slid toward the open grave—the vault cover swerved, angled downward severely, and its corner collided with the casket below.

I shrieked. My vision blurred. Ron's sister rushed forward to shield us. I stood paralyzed as the backhoe righted itself and reversed slowly away from the grave. I heard someone behind me say that the coffin hadn't been punctured. The four of us huddled even closer to each other. "This is a sign Laura doesn't want to leave us," our rabbi improvised. The heavy slab was then lifted again, and—by hand—workers guided it into place.

At our rabbi's cue, Ron pulled a nearby shovel out of the frozen earth. By tradition, covering a casket with the first shovelfuls of dirt is a sign of respect for the deceased; it's also supposed to signify the last burial rite before the mourning period begins. Our rabbi recited more prayers as Ron shoveled three scoops of dirt onto the coffin. Then it was my turn. I gripped the shovel and, in a daze, tossed more earth into the grave. I passed the shovel to Sara. Sara passed it to Rachel.

We returned to the limousine. The girls and our parents climbed in, but Ron and I stayed outside, watching the cemetery workers slowly fill Laura's grave. Shivering, I balanced on one foot and then the other as my feet burned from the cold. "I can't watch anymore," I finally declared with a moan. "I'm freezing. I'm done." Ron put his arm around me and guided me into the limousine. I removed my boots and rubbed my throbbing feet.

I pushed away the thought of Laura's body below the earth.

We were headed to our synagogue to sit *shiva*—the Jewish custom where the immediate family of the deceased opens up their home, for a period of up to seven nights, so mourners can pay respects. However, Margie had convinced us our synagogue's community hall could better handle the expected crowd, as well as allow us to preserve our home as an escape from the well-meaning but overwhelming attention.

A few of Sara and Rachel's friends approached them as we

entered the hall. They went off together to an empty classroom. I was glad the girls could avoid the adult responsibility of receiving condolences; they knew many of the mourners from our community, but others—Ron's colleagues; Jewish community volunteers; Laura's classmates, friends, and their parents—would be strangers to them. They didn't need any more stress on this already overwhelming and traumatic day.

The line snaked outside the community hall and into the hallway. We consoled the mourners as they consoled us. I wondered why their eyes, not mine, filled with tears. Many guests understood the devastating extent of our loss more profoundly than I did in that moment; all that surrounded me seemed distorted, far away. I wondered how I could be sitting *shiva* for Laura. How was this possible?

I sensed fear as the mourners offered us their condolences, especially on the faces of mothers whose children were the same age as Laura or those with only one child. They listened to my endless stream of words, words that coated my frazzled nerves and prevented me from falling apart.

I felt distant, almost like an observer. As we accepted the condolences, I was hugging and talking to friends, but as if for a different purpose—more like I was welcoming guests in a wedding receiving line. Toward the back of the room, friends and family mingled around the long buffet table; it seemed odd not to be with them. A sea of voices offered their sympathies as I received each mourner:

"I'm so sorry, Susan."

"Laura was such a wonderful girl."

"I can't imagine what you're going through."

"What can I do for you?"

A friend who had recently undergone both a mastectomy and a hysterectomy approached me. "Susan, I'm so sorry, but I'm glad Laura didn't have to suffer," she said. She then explained that the side effects from radiation and chemotherapy were so awful that at times she'd wanted to die.

Shocked by her candidness yet wanting to hear more, I braced myself and leaned in closer to her. It hit me for the first time: had Laura lived, her prognosis wouldn't have been good. Chemotherapy, radiation, and their potentially devastating side effects—nausea, hair loss, learning disabilities, infertility—would've been real possibilities. While the initial MRI had been hopeful, we'd later learned that Laura's tumor was malignant and probably not survivable. My mind reeled. Seeing Laura suffer for weeks or even months only to die would have been worse.

The next day, before we returned to the synagogue for the second night of *shiva*, I found myself surrounded at home by two of my college friends and three of Ron's—all of whom had flown to Milwaukee, on extremely short notice, to be with us. They listened patiently as I retold each of them, in individual, no-holds-barred conversations, every miserable, frightening, surreal detail of the last week. I talked to reframe the events, to understand them, to integrate them into my new reality, to stay sane. I talked to lighten the heaviness in my chest and ease the acidity in my stomach. I talked to keep Laura with me. I talked to try and reorder my world—the sense of predictability and control I'd always thrived on was gone forever.

Blurring condolences and stories of classmates' special relationships with Laura filled the next two evenings of the *shiva*. A senior who'd worked with Laura on the school newspaper told me how impressed he'd been with her motivation and freshman writing skills. Another young man told me how he'd looked forward each day to talking to Laura in their science class. And one of her girlfriends described how, on the day of the funeral, Nicolet High School's hallways had been a sea of pink—Laura's favorite color.

We also learned that many of Laura's classmates had received our family's announcement during the finale of the high school's musical, *Hello Dolly*. A friend of mine, a parent who had attended the performance, told me that, just as the curtain came down to a standing ovation, she'd heard a sob from a girl at the back of the theater. "The news spread like a wave in slow motion," she said. Students immediately gathered in the foyer and the parking lot, and parents invited kids into their homes so they could be together to process the news.

During one of these days—I can't remember which—a *Milwaukee Journal Sentinel* reporter left a voicemail for Ron. Laura's sudden death was rare enough to be newsworthy, especially since the cancer that took her afflicts fewer than five hundred children in the US annually.[2] To avoid more publicity, Ron initially debated whether he should call the reporter back, but we also knew the story would be written with or without our input.

The article, "Ambitious Girl, 14, Didn't Know Meaning of the Word 'No,'" described Laura as an old soul, with an understanding and appreciation for life far beyond her years. Laura's English teacher was quoted: "If anybody could believe her way into something, it was Laura. She had the talent and the ability, but also the vision—and those are things you can't teach." Ron

2. See <www.cancer.net/cancer-types/medulloblastoma-childhood/statistics> for more information.

was quoted as saying, "She had her own path and her own self-confidence. She had a sense of justice. [...] She was a fourteen-year gift to each and every one of us."

The article was well done, but Laura was so much more than that.

On Wednesday evening, after the third and last night of the *shiva*, our family—the four of us—returned to our eerily quiet house. We were all exhausted and drained, and thankfully Sara and Rachel both fell asleep as soon as we tucked them in. Ron and I crawled into bed early, too. Within moments, Ron suddenly pulled away from me, buried his face in his pillow, and began sobbing. I'd only seen him cry once in our twenty years of marriage, when his grandmother had died. Those had been silent tears of sadness, but this was different. He was overcome by emotion, struggling for breath and sobbing as I'd never seen before.

"Keep strong," I thought to myself as I dried my own tears. "It's his turn. If we both break apart, we'll drown." Yet there was too little I could do to comfort him—this loss was too great. I pressed my hand into his back as his tears streamed freely. When his desolate sobs began to lesson, I brought him an Ambien (which had been prescribed the day before), and he soon fell into a deep, much-needed sleep.

Tangled thoughts and a nauseous fear gripped me as I lay in the dark. I felt alone, uncertain, confused. I picked up the phone on my nightstand but then paused. Margie had been a constant presence since Wednesday; her help and emotional support had been invaluable. Was it right to ask for anything more? It was 11:00 p.m. on a school night, and I debated if I should call.

Finally, I dialed her number. "Margie, I can't sleep. I can't make sense of what's happened. I'm lost, I don't know what to do.

I feel like I'm going crazy." Margie practically read my mind as she replied, "I'll be over in fifteen minutes."

I closed the bedroom door behind me, relieved that I could let Ron sleep. A few minutes later, I watched as Margie came up the walkway and the headlights from her son's car left our driveway. I answered the door in my pajamas. Margie followed me into the den where I covered myself with a blanket and hugged my legs to my chest. She crossed her legs and waited for me to begin.

My voice raced to untangle my whirling thoughts and emotions. With all sense of control stripped away, I craved information: I wanted to learn more about our community's conversations, events, and reactions. Margie told me all she could and assured me that our friends, in their collective grief, wanted to help us in any way possible. She reminded me that Laura had not suffered, that her death had been unpreventable. I wanted—with all my heart—to believe her.

"That's what we can't get out of our minds," I said. "If we'd taken Laura's headaches more seriously, if we'd brought her to the doctor sooner, would she still be with us? How could I have let her go to school when she was in pain?" I asked many, many questions, questions that had no answers. Margie listened.

After talking for two hours, I rubbed my eyes. "I don't know what we would've done without your help, Margie." I hugged her as I got up from the couch. "I'll stay down here," she assured me.

I felt lighter as I climbed the stairs. Talking had lessened, however temporarily, the pain churning inside of me. I now realized we would need to accept help from our wider circle of friends, as well as from our community at large. The challenges ahead would be too overwhelming to handle ourselves.

CHAPTER 6

Our New World

March 2009

Laura's death undercut our most basic life assumptions—we were good parents who loved and protected our children, and yet our firstborn had received a life-threatening diagnosis and died, essentially, within a day. I now lived in a world I didn't recognize, a warped yet too-real reality. Somehow, the minutes ticked by as usual, as if nothing out of the ordinary had happened. The Earth still rotated, and as the basics of daily life went on, I cringed at this bizarreness—how could life ever be normal without all five of us together?

It was now the weekend when Sara's *bat mitzvah* should have taken place. Ron's cousins Rena and Jeff—both doctors in San Francisco—had kept their originally scheduled flights to Milwaukee. "My chest feels heavy," I complained to Rena. "I don't feel good. My left shoulder feels weird, too." She explained that grief and heartache can sometimes mimic the symptoms of a heart attack. She took my pulse and instructed me to lie down on the couch and take deep breaths. Although she assured me I would be fine, I didn't completely believe her. Only a week ago, I'd learned all too well that doctors are severely limited when it comes to predicting (or controlling) their patients' outcomes. I tried to believe what Rena was telling me, though, because it was what I needed to hear. Not so much for myself, but for Sara, Rachel, and Ron—our family couldn't handle another crisis.

In the days after the *shiva*, Ron focused on logistics; he'd sorted through the piles of condolence cards, newspaper articles, and boxes of the funeral home's preprinted thank-you notes. He'd also tackled the details of Sara's canceled *bat mitzvah* party—the DJ, caterer, florist, and photographer were all very understanding. I was thankful that Ron had handled these responsibilities since I felt utterly incapable of focusing on anything other than our grief. I took comfort in knowing that taking charge was how Ron managed his sadness.

Ron and I firmly believed that the only way to move forward was to reclaim as much of our lives as possible—no matter how daunting that seemed—and to do so as soon as possible. One week after Laura's funeral, Sara and Rachel went back to school. Sara had told us that she wanted to be with her classmates, and Rachel, nestling on the couch with her favorite blanket by her side, had been watching far too many *SpongeBob SquarePants* episodes. Ron chose to return to the office later that week. What good would cloistering ourselves do? The longer we waited to emerge from the cocoon of our home, the harder it would be for all of us to face the world.

By 8:00 a.m. on Wednesday morning, I was alone in the kitchen. An anguished numbness prickled my skin and muddled my brain. The refrigerator hummed. A bird flew by the window. The bare tree branches swayed, the crystal-blue February sky mocked me. I wanted to crawl outside of my body and follow Laura to where she was. I couldn't imagine living the next four or five decades without her. I felt guilty for living when she had not.

The four of us ate, slept, and made decisions based on our gut instincts, all under a hazy cloud. I began fixating on Sara's canceled *bat mitzvah* and started thinking about how we could reschedule her ceremony. Even in our shock and sadness, Ron and I feared that Sara's connection to Judaism might be weakened, or even irreparably damaged, if she didn't become a *bat mitzvah*. Being welcomed into the Jewish community as an adult was too significant a milestone for her to miss.

We'd initially believed that Sara had lost her opportunity to read her assigned Torah portion, which she'd spent the past four months studying and practicing. (Torah portions, fifty-four in total, are read throughout the year in chronological order; with a few exceptions, each portion corresponds to a specific week.) I soon realized, however, that since Sara's *bat mitzvah* had been scheduled at a less-traditional, late-Saturday-afternoon *Havdalah* time, her portion could also be recited on the following Saturday morning, March 7th. Ron liked the idea and Sara agreed, even though a celebration of any kind under these circumstances seemed far from normal.

We worked with our rabbi and cantor. Arranging the ceremony on such short notice gave us something—other than our heartache—to focus on, while also ensuring that we met Sara's needs. We invited about three dozen family and friends, all of whom had been to Laura's funeral—a few of the guests had even been pallbearers. I didn't know if we were doing the right thing, but choosing to do *something* was better than doing nothing.

On the day of Sara's *bat mitzvah*, I felt disconnected from reality as she chanted her Torah portion in our synagogue's small chapel. Just over two weeks ago, we'd held Laura's funeral in the larger sanctuary, and yet here we were celebrating Sara's milestone: two events, two daughters, two weeks, two very different ceremonies. I alternated between glancing at friends and family and wondering what they were feeling, to gazing at the floor to avoid their baffled, bittersweet expressions. All of these people had rearranged their lives and schedules once again to be here for us and bear witness to Sara's rite of passage. I willed myself not to cry, placed my arm around Rachel, and hugged her closer to me.

At twelve-and-a-half years old, Sara displayed a maturity that still amazes me. Not only did she chant her Torah and *haftarah* portions beautifully, but at the end of the service, she also spoke a few sentences about her relationship with Laura. Their roles had been upended: instead of Sara talking about Laura on this special occasion, Laura should've been sharing anecdotes about Sara and voicing her love for her younger sister. To this day, I remain proud of Sara for her bravery and resilience.

Following the service, we invited our guests to join us at a nearby Italian restaurant for lunch. We needed their support as well as the distraction—it would've been weird and anti-climactic to go home immediately after the ceremony. Sara, too, deserved to have her special day commemorated, especially since we had to postpone the *bat mitzvah* party we'd planned for her. Even though we could only offer Sara a small celebration on her big day, the afternoon provided a pleasant, needed respite from our grief. Yet in the end, we still had to return to our own home, a house filled with Laura's absence.

Nights were the hardest. While Ron and I could keep ourselves distractedly busy during the day, when the lights went out, the irreversibility of death was inescapable. Each night, I visualized a maze of "what ifs," all of which slammed into a stone wall: What if Laura's pediatrician had ordered an MRI after her first neurological exam? What if I'd insisted that Laura be placed in the ICU when her tumor was first diagnosed? What if Laura, wherever she was, blamed us for her death?

As parents, we had done everything we were supposed to do, yet in the end we were powerless. Again and again, I agonized over our being able to protect Sara and Rachel. Headlines screamed in my mind: "Rare Brain Cancer Strikes Down Three Sisters." Despite the doctors having assured us that Laura's tumor was not genetic, I now knew that doctors could be wrong. Were our surviving daughters at risk? What were we supposed to do now? Which rules should we follow to keep them safe? For the first time in my life, I knew that none exist.

I tried to talk myself out of my anguish. Laura had suffered from the incredibly rare bad luck of cancer cells in her cerebellum, which had likely multiplied out of control throughout her childhood. By the time the tumor started causing headaches, it had already become fatal. If it had been diagnosed any earlier, Ron and I—and Laura—would've spent months in anguish. We would've had to confront horrific medical decisions, many which probably would've been dictated by doctors; our ability to refuse treatments for Laura would've been limited, regardless of how painful, invasive, or futile they might have been.

If Laura had undergone her originally-scheduled surgery, Ron and I would have been forced to split our time between staying at the hospital and caring for our two other daughters. Sara and Rachel would've had to watch as their sister's condition deteriorated—something potentially even scarier and more traumatic for them. Yet for all that turmoil and pain, and even though we might have had a few more weeks or months together, Laura still would've died. To this day, I still become overwhelmed thinking about parents across the country who sit at the bedsides of their terminally-ill children, praying for them to survive yet knowing they will not.

I convinced myself that the suddenness of Laura's passing was the lesser of two evils. Laura had no reason to be afraid—she didn't know the end of her life was imminent, and Ron and I were saved from having to explain her terminal illness to her. She didn't suffer, and we were spared the anguish of watching her in pain. And, although we hadn't been able to say a true goodbye, I can't imagine what either of us would've said other than, "I love you." Laura already knew how deeply we cherished her, because we'd told her as much on a daily basis, with both our words and actions. We had no regrets about our relationship with her; there were no wounds to repair or rifts to mend.

Yet no matter how hard I tried to talk myself down each night, I still felt deprived. Deprived of Laura—nothing was more painful than that—but also deprived of the life I'd been raised to expect, almost promised. Why hadn't following the rules and striving to be a good person protected my family and me from adversity? And what could possibly happen to us next? Ron—or Sara or Rachel—could die too: then what would I do? I'd now have to live the rest of my life worrying about another tragedy blindsiding us. No amount of doing good or striving for perfection would ever shield us.

I tried to focus on the good Ron and I still had in our lives: we still had two healthy daughters, and we still had each other. Ron's job allowed him flexibility as did my volunteering. We had the benefit of being connected to our community through our daughters' schools, our synagogue, our volunteering, and Ron's colleagues. Our network of friends would continue offering us both emotional and practical assistance, I was sure of that much.

"It's like Laura was killed in a car crash, not from cancer," Ron said as we went to bed one night. "It feels like we've been robbed of a third of our future, a third of our life." I spent the next hour or two awake in the dark: he was right. We'd assumed Laura would have a bright future and a long life, and we'd done our best to prepare her for adulthood. We'd encouraged her creativity, her strengths, her dreams. We'd looked forward to teaching her to drive, giving her dating advice, celebrating when she graduated from high school, and bringing her on college tours. As Laura started a career, got married, and had children of her own, we'd expected to be full of pride at every turn.

In a sense, Laura's loss of life was ours as well. We'd now become "younger" parents: we would have to wait at least two more years before Sara or Rachel would reach these milestones. We would remain stuck on our board-game square while other parents moved ahead without us. I thought about the joyous, countless hours we'd put into parenting Laura; I hoped I could find the energy to continue investing the same amount of effort into Sara and Rachel. They deserved no less, but I wasn't sure, as I lay in the dark, that I had the strength to give it to them.

My chest tightened as I thought of Laura and all the snuggles we'd shared with her in this very bed. My not-so-subtle groans woke Ron up. I cringed and turned on my side, away from him. From behind, Ron hugged me with an intensity that took me by surprise. Tears slid silently down my cheeks and onto my neck and pillow.

CHAPTER 7

Facing Forward

Spring 2009

The Monday morning after Sara's *bat mitzvah* ceremony, I went upstairs after breakfast to get dressed. I walked by my unmade bed. I considered climbing in and pulling the crumpled covers over my head, but if I did that, I might never come out again. People would understand, I thought, if I retreated from life, but if I became a depressed hermit, what would that accomplish? I couldn't do that to our family. I needed to keep moving for their sake as well as my own.

"You'll smile again one day," a friend had assured me a few days earlier. She intended her comment to be uplifting and hopeful, but her low expectation for our future happiness had disturbed and scared me: Would the occasional joyful moment be the most we could hope for from now on? If we functioned better than "expected," did that mean we were being disloyal to Laura or callous about her death? Should we be miserable all the time? What was expected of a grieving family, a grieving mom? And why did I still care so much about what others thought?

I picked up my phone and looked at my calendar. I was scheduled to attend a transition-planning meeting at the MJF the next day. Just three months earlier (in December), I'd accepted the nomination to become the president of the MJF's Women's Division. My term was set to begin in May, but now, with our lives in upheaval and grief looming over us, how could I justify taking on this demanding and public role?

I stared down at the calendar and understood what was at stake. Now more than ever, I needed to stay connected to the community that made Milwaukee our home. Isolating myself in the house every day, with my tangled thoughts and sadness, would be agonizing. I'd be better off continuing with my work and surrounding myself with women who cared about me. I didn't want to be defined as "the mom who lost a daughter." I still wanted the purpose and meaning that my volunteer career provided, and I still wanted to help others. I thought of how hard I'd worked since becoming a volunteer: I was determined not to lose this piece of myself.

I reflected on the times, over the years, when I'd been embarrassed when I was asked what I did for a living. I usually mumbled in reply, "I volunteer and have three young children." I wished, in retrospect, that I'd answered with more confidence: "I assist nonprofits with their fundraising, marketing, and leadership programs, and I parent three daughters." Just because I didn't receive a paycheck didn't mean my work was any less important than any other career, or any less rewarding. I should've been prouder of the work I did to help others. I should've been prouder of being a role model for my daughters.

Serving as president, I realized, was no longer feasible for me just now; I would have to talk with Evy—my longtime mentor and the Women's Division staff coordinator—as well as the outgoing president about my options going forward. Both would undoubtedly understand and respect my decision. I trusted that

Evy and the other leaders would help me find a less-intensive but still-involved role.

The next afternoon, I located my keys under a pile of condolence cards and got in my minivan, which I hadn't driven for the past two weeks. Certainly, under the circumstances, no one would expect me to be at this meeting, but I gave myself permission to attend. Yet, just as I got in the elevator at the Federation's offices, a tightness seized my chest and throat. I questioned my decision as many doubts flew into my mind. Was I going back too soon? Was I doing the right thing? How would the other volunteers react to me?

I paused outside the conference room door as I listened to the lighthearted chatting on the other side. I debated getting back in the elevator before anybody noticed me. Turning back seemed tempting—and much less stressful—but I steadied myself and opened the door.

Idy, the outgoing president, was the first person who saw me. Her eyes widened as if she'd seen a ghost. "I shouldn't have come," I thought. But as Idy moved toward me, her stunned look transformed into an empathetic smile, and she greeted me with a hug. The other dozen or so women, almost all of whom had been to Laura's funeral or *shiva*, expressed how happy they were to see me.

My shoulders relaxed and the heaviness in my chest lifted: I was where I needed to be. Going back to my volunteer work didn't mean I needed to stop grieving, didn't mean I was disrespecting all that Laura meant to me. Rather, it meant I could rely on this community of women and trust that they would offer their support. And that's exactly what happened: in the months to come, they would listen as I recounted, over and over again, the days leading up to and following Laura's death. They would be there to hear my pain as I journeyed on a daunting, uncertain path.

***

In the evenings, Ron and I read through the posts on the CaringBridge website, as well as on Laura's still-active Facebook page (and on our own pages). The posts numbered in the hundreds and were a powerful albeit temporary balm. These virtual healing spaces were a godsend: without social media, we never would've seen these messages, nor would friends and family have had a place where they could instantly feel close to others who were also mourning Laura.

Messages of sympathy overflowed our mailbox as well. Each day, when I checked our roadside mailbox, a stack of condolence cards awaited me. Many days, cards in hand, I cried as I drove down our driveway to the house. As I ripped each envelope open, I wondered about what I'd find inside. I was grateful for each and every person who took the time to acknowledge our loss, but I especially cherished the cards with stories about Laura—these shared memories became poor but treasured substitutes for the absence of future ones. We looked forward to receiving the cards each day, and each night the girls would guess how many more would arrive the next day. Each evening, Ron would place the cards in Laura's memory box.

Reordering our lives without Laura became the new normal, but still my brain lagged behind reality, like a bruise which doesn't immediately emerge. Some days I would try to pretend Laura was away at camp, or perhaps at a sleepover, but these tactics rarely worked for long: I'd never been good at playing make-believe. When shopping for groceries, I continued buying Laura's favorites—guacamole, peach yogurt, cranberry juice, chicken and dumpling soup—but then, days later, I would wonder why they remained untouched. Sometimes I'd walk into the house half-expecting to see Laura at the kitchen table, only to have reality slam down on me once more. While getting ready for bed one evening, I looked out into the hall and glimpsed a blur of pink—a Victoria's Secret sweatshirt and pastel-striped pajama pants. For a split second, lightness surged through my chest as Laura came skipping toward me. Time stopped, and all seemed right with the world. In the next instant, I recognized Sara's beautiful brown eyes and shivered at my mistake; she was wearing Laura's favorite pajamas. "What's wrong, Mom?" Sara asked. I tried to hide my shock as I hugged her tightly.

Ron spent many evenings organizing Laura's things. We scoured Laura's computer together, looking for selfies she'd taken with her friends and cousins, as well as for her creative-writing pieces. We found many school essays—some of which we'd never seen before—and more than one graphic-design file with her name stylized in her favorite fonts. Ron began collecting Laura's writings, pictures, and fashion sketches so he could bind them together, along with countless condolence notes, into a scrapbook; once finished, he planned to give copies to Sara, Rachel, and our parents. The more recent pictures of Laura, especially the ones we'd taken on our winter trip to Israel, reminded me of how oblivious we'd been to the cancerous cells multiplying in the base of her brain, how unaware we'd been of the short amount of time we had left with her.

Much like with the funeral and burial, Ron attacked logistics with startling efficiency—his attempt at managing his grief, his way of putting on a brave face for Sara and Rachel. I never appreciated his energy more, but my heart sank the afternoon

I discovered he'd disconnected Laura's phone and had lost her sweet voicemail prompt in the process. "Why didn't you ask me before you did that?" I snapped. "We had to cancel it at some point," Ron answered before adding defensively, "It's too late to get it back now. There's nothing we can do." He didn't apologize, but I could tell he was sorry.

I narrowed my eyes at him and clasped my hands around the back of my neck. Upstairs in our bedroom, I tried to calm myself down. I remained upset for the rest of the evening, but it was useless to be angry at him for any longer. We needed to be on the same team, needed to rely on each other's strength.

Ron had action to help him cope, but I still wanted a road-map—a step-by-step guide on what to do when your fourteen-year-old daughter dies without warning. At some point, I even went to a local bookstore and scanned the grief section, but the books—covered with pastel butterflies and flowers—depressed me. I didn't need sentimental poems or coddling, I needed a plan. Why wasn't there a plan?

In the early years of our marriage, Ron had been surprised by my crying spells, which were a holdover from when I was a teenager. Whenever too much angst built up inside of me, I'd escape to our bedroom and cry until I hit the bottom of my misery. The release allowed me to regain control, to recharge my usual optimism. But now there was no bottom and I was overwhelmed by even simple, everyday tasks. In the shadow of Laura's death, I feared melting into a puddle of pity; I was afraid I would be utterly drained of the energy I needed to parent Sara and Rachel.

I willed myself to remain in control as much as possible, to show Ron I was strong so I could believe it myself. Creating stability was what Ron and I, in our twenty years of marriage, did well together. We had silently made a pact: we refused to sacrifice our surviving daughters' futures for what couldn't be undone.

Reclaiming stability was now our main priority, yet I felt utterly and unrelentingly robbed of Laura and her beautiful aura. An unnatural vacuum. A black hole. A void. An absence of presence. A distance that seemed just a bit more expansive with each passing day. One night, when the nightly, stern-sounding public service announcement, "Do you know where your children are?" aired before the news, I had to stop myself from screaming in reply, "No, I don't know where Laura is! And what would you like me to do about that?" On a separate afternoon, as I was driving to pick up Rachel from school, a well-known medium came on the radio. I was instantly transfixed—as a child I'd been fascinated by the paranormal and mystified by afterlife experiences. Now I felt drawn to anyone who could connect me to Laura in any way. I hoped the medium could tell me where Laura was and if she was at peace. I pulled over to the side of the road and debated calling the show, but the program ended before I could summon the courage.

When several friends—without our specifically asking for recommendations—independently suggested the same family grief counselor, Ron and I agreed to reach out to her. Two weeks later, on a weeknight evening, we invited Laurie to our home. Ron and I discussed possibilities for ongoing therapy sessions before introducing Sara and Rachel to her. After several minutes of awkward introductions, they escaped to the den and back to their television show. I couldn't blame them—a grief counselor in our living room must have seemed intrusive and scary. I wondered if we should handle our grief without relying on a therapist, as my parents almost certainly would have. My gut told me we had to do what felt right for us, and I could see no real reason to go it alone. Why shouldn't we ask for help?

Before my first therapy session with Laurie, I scanned the sparsely-filled waiting room and hoped no one would recognize me. I'd never thought of myself as someone who needed therapy, and I tried to suppress embarrassment; if Laura were alive, I rationalized, I would have no reason to be here. I reassured myself that counseling would help me manage my feelings and accept the finality of death. I had no control over losing Laura and no way of getting her back, but maybe I could learn how to survive in a world without her.

I moved to a more private seating area, nearer to Laurie's office, and removed a blank journal from my purse. Ever since I'd been given a diary for my thirteenth birthday, recording my innermost reflections and emotions had been a part of my life, something I'd always enjoyed doing. I began to scribble down Laura's traits, habits, and idiosyncrasies—I feared I would forget or block these memories if I didn't record them. I was afraid I would forget to celebrate Laura's life in the midst of mourning her death.

As I wrote, I was haunted by my inability, years earlier, to complete Laura's baby book. My perfectionism—which made me believe I wouldn't do the project justice—had hindered me from filling in the blank branches of the family tree, creating photo collages, and recording each "first." To make it easier for myself, I'd bought a baby calendar with printed stickers—first smile, first sentence, first steps—that I used to record each milestone. I'd always been a bit frustrated with myself for not completing her baby book, although I'd been better about saving all three of the girls' hospital identification bracelets, maternity ward photos, preschool artwork, and other important keepsakes. Every few years, I also handwrote letters to each of them, in which I described their evolving and distinct personalities and my love for them.

As I waited, I wrote about Laura's adoring the *Madeline* book series; her fondness for the colloquialism, "Home is where the heart is"; the occasional "garage sales" all three girls held to trade their prized possessions; the multi-day Monopoly marathons that Laura instigated. As I jotted down my memories I imagined the two of us rummaging through clothing racks at Forever 21, Laura sharing the highlights of her day when I picked her up from school, and her humming along to her favorite songs on the car radio. My skin prickled as I visualized our eating lunch at a Potbelly restaurant—less than one month earlier—and talking about her plans for the summer. I smiled when I remembered that Laura had ordered her favorite salad that day and had asked, as usual, for extra cranberries.

In Laurie's office, with a glass of water on the end table and a tissue in my hand, I longed to hear about how other moms who had lost a daughter had coped; I hoped their stories might be the roadmap I needed. Instead, Laurie shared general coping strategies and anecdotes from other clients. She told me there was no one way to mourn, no right or wrong way to manage the heartache, no specific healing time frame. She reminded me that each death, and each grieving experience, differs vastly. Most importantly, Laurie told me that although none of us had been given a choice in Laura's death, we didn't need to allow loss to define us.

I talked with Laurie about my overwhelming, always-lurking fears for Sara and Rachel's health and safety, even though they seemed less worried about their own health than I would've predicted. As for me, Laura's death had made me alarmist. Many nights, typically in the wee hours, I'd bolt upright in bed with an impending sense of dread. I'd walk down the hall and nudge open Sara and Rachel's bedroom doors, then stand motionless waiting to hear them breathe. Only when they rolled over would I crawl back into bed. (Ron did the same on many nights, too.) I told Laurie about one evening when Sara had gone out with friends and I'd fallen asleep waiting to hear her come in. Hours later, I'd awoken in a panic: Where was Sara? Was she hurt? Had the police been unable to reach us? I'd jumped out of bed and flown down the hallway only to find Sara safe and sound in her room, curled up under her comforter and fast asleep.

Laurie assured me that my anxiety—and so many other feelings—were a normal part of shock, of mourning. The grief would be more manageable, she advised, if my family and I followed the HALT strategy—to avoid, as much as possible, letting ourselves become too Hungry, Angry, Lonely, or Tired. We discussed the benefits of exercise, afternoon naps, and conversations with friends. She suggested that we buy a punching bag so we could release our anger constructively. I agreed with these common-sense recommendations and promised to implement them. As I would soon find out, many of these techniques proved surprisingly effective on some days and utterly useless on others. The punching bag, which Ron immediately installed on the unfinished side of the basement, would rarely be used.

In my weekly sessions with Laurie, I talked more in monologue than conversation. My words compelled my brain to believe the unbelievable, to reframe my identity, to reconcile the four worst days of my life with reality. Ron and I were, in many ways, still the same people we'd been on the Tuesday before Laura was rushed to the hospital. Sorrow and loss would now always be a part of us, but that didn't mean our resilience had been stolen from us, too.

When I talked with Laurie, I often felt more like a detached storyteller than how I imagined a grieving mom "should be." I felt guilty about not being distraught all the time, guilty because I could disengage from the intensity of my anguish at times—in fact, there were surprisingly frequent windows when I could "forget," laugh, or enjoy time with friends in the moment. I eventually admitted my festering shame: "I thought I would be more devastated, more miserable," I told Laurie. "Susan, don't worry," she replied. "It's normal. You're still in shock. Those feelings will come soon enough."

And then they did. Weeks later, when my body's initial, protective dose of adrenaline had dissipated, a wave of depression hit me: without Laura, I was diminished, my identity altered, no longer whole. I spent a few days lost in a low before forcing myself to re-engage with life in a meaningful way. Later on, I would begin having high-functioning days where our new normal felt simply normal, but waves of sorrow would again consume me every few days. When these feelings would hit, the brutal finality of never being with Laura again stripped me of my breath and purpose.

I told Laurie how hard the nights were, of the nightmarish emptiness I'd often wake up to. In the dark, Ron would remind me that Laura's cancer was not hereditary, and that the odds of two brain tumors in one family were infinitesimal. After reassuring me time and time again, Ron would often hold me until I fell back asleep. He made me feel safer and calmer. His steadiness anchored me when self-pity threatened to sweep me away; he gave me the strength I needed to set an example for Sara and Rachel as they navigated their own sea of emotions.

My fifty-five-minute therapy sessions would often end too soon for me. At the end of each appointment, Laurie would guide me toward the door and praise me for how well our family was managing. I soaked up her compliments; they refueled me. I viewed falling apart as failure and wanted to exceed expectations, and my breaking apart would've meant disappointing my family and friends. Following each session, I would pause on the landing outside of Laurie's second-floor office, take a deep breath, and steel myself against the emotional struggles of the upcoming week.

CHAPTER 8

Glimpses of Growth:
Organ Donation

Spring 2009

Passover was our first major holiday without Laura. As we drove the ninety minutes to Evanston to celebrate *Seder* with our families, I glanced at the backseat. Sara and Rachel were both asleep, each of their heads resting on a different door. The middle seat was conspicuously empty.

Seated around the dining table at my parents' home—with Ron's parents, and my sister and her family—we took turns reading the story about the Israelites escaping slavery in Egypt and wandering the desert for forty years before reaching the promised land of Israel. Passover's story and symbols, which I'd always accepted at face value, now took on new meanings: the Israelites' passage from slavery to freedom made me reflect on our family's opposite journey—from peace to strife, contentment to grief. As we took turns recounting the ten plagues that Moses delivered to Pharaoh—such as boils, locusts, and three days of darkness—I dipped my finger into my wine glass and placed a drop onto my plate. This tradition symbolizes the lessening of joy as the wine is removed from the glass, but the wine drop is also a symbol of how each generation experiences its own adversities—of the resilience of the Jewish people. When it came time for me to read the final plague—the slaying of the firstborn—its significance to our own family's story hit me. I swallowed hard and looked in shock at Ron. The word *Passover*, from the Hebrew *Pesach*, refers to the death-plague that passed over the Israelites' homes and spared the eldest child within each. We had not escaped such a fate.

The *Pesach* meal is both symbolic and ritualistic. Each food on the *Seder* plate has a meaning and is eaten at a specific time and in a certain order. At the appropriate time, I broke off two pieces of *matzah* (unleavened bread) and combined the *haroset* (crushed apples and walnuts with sweet wine) with the *maror* (bitter horseradish) to create a Hillel sandwich. The clashing flavors symbolize life's bitter and sweet aspects; as I ate, it was impossible for me to avoid thinking about our family's own complex, often intermingling emotions.

I stared at the one empty chair at the dining table—a seat saved, per tradition, to welcome the prophet Elijah—and I wondered why a seat hadn't been saved for Laura as well. The meal was intensely awkward: we received looks of pity, but I don't remember anybody mentioning Laura, specifically saying how much she was missed, or even asking how we were coping. Talking to others about losing Laura, especially to those who lived the story with us, was my lifeline; this Passover, I felt isolated in my grief. Anger swelled inside of me. I stayed at the table for as long as I could before going to the bathroom and wiping away the tears I'd been struggling to hold back. I spent the rest of the meal wandering through the house and thinking about how Laura had played with her sisters and cousins in these rooms less than two months before. I sensed Laura's presence but wondered if I were the only one who still felt that connection. Is this what holidays would become now? Celebrations full of mundane chitchat as if Laura had never existed?

I was too annoyed and hurt to mention the one piece of hopeful news I'd wanted to talk more about with our families: we'd recently learned from Emily, the organ-donor coordinator, that Laura's liver had been placed with a teacher in upstate New York. Placing an organ with someone who lived so far away was unusual, according to Emily, because of strict protocols for organ donation dictated by the United Network for Organ Sharing (UNOS), which regulates transplant waiting lists, organ donation, and procurement.[3] When a match for Laura's liver hadn't been found in Wisconsin, the search was expanded to the Midwest and then to other regions. When Ron had initially told me about Emily's call, even in my fog of shock and grief, I remember having felt a tiny glimmer of hope—perhaps something good came from our decision to donate Laura's organs.

We learned more about the recipient of Laura's liver through a letter we received in early May. Although donor families and organ recipients are governed by confidentiality rules during the first year after a transplant, both are allowed to communicate anonymously by mail with the help of organ-sharing networks. When we'd received our letter (with the recipient's identifying information redacted), I had trouble grasping what I was reading. At first, I thought the letter was the Wisconsin Donor Network's standard thank-you note, something sent to all donor families regardless of whether or not the donated organ(s) had been transplanted. Ron, Sara, and Rachel refused to join me in my unfounded skepticism, and when I read the letter again, I realized

---

3. See <https://unos.org/transplantation/matching-organs> for more information.

they were right. The words on the page, even with so much information blacked out, were sincere and specific:

April 22, 2009

Dear Donor Family,

My name is [redacted]. I am a forty-year-old special education teacher. I work with children in kindergarten and first grade in [redacted]. I love my job! I also love fitness. I teach aerobics almost daily and play soccer and volleyball. Although I have many hobbies, my true love is family and friends.

[Redacted.]

[Redacted.] I was placed at the top of the donor list due to the severity of my case.

On Sunday, February 22, exactly two months ago today, I was given the gift of life. There are no words to explain how grateful I am to your family. I know this must be hard for you, and for that I am so very sorry. I want you to know that I cherish each and every day to the fullest. I am healing nicely and hope to get back to all my normal daily routines soon.

Now that I'm feeling better, I am starting to work on my goal of increasing organ donation. Your gift to me is a miracle, and I want to be able to help others with miracles. Again, I want to thank you from the bottom of my heart. I would love to hear from you and maybe even meet you someday.

For me, it was enough to know that Laura's liver had saved someone's life and that we'd played a part in this miracle. I didn't initially feel as if I needed to connect with this woman, but Ron, Sara, and Rachel felt otherwise; they dismissed my concerns about sharing our information with a virtual stranger. With my eventual approval, and with the assistance of the Wisconsin and New York Donor Networks, Ron sent pictures of Laura and our family to the recipient, along with a note from Sara and Rachel. Although Ron and I helped them compose their letter, I'm still amazed by the maturity and honesty our daughters conveyed, especially in their closing lines:

> We cannot tell you how happy we are that we were able to save your life. We miss Laura so much, but knowing that she saved your life helps lessen some of the pain.
>
> It's still hard to understand that our sister's death helped save you. We can only imagine the impact our choice has made on your friends, family, and community. You are proof that miracles do happen and that some good can come out of tragedies. We hope everyone hears our story and decides to become an organ donor.

I remember how strongly the girls—Sara in particular—had felt about donating Laura's organs. In truth, they were the ones who ultimately persuaded Ron and me to consent to the donation: instead of focusing on their own pain, Sara and Rachel were thinking about how we, as a family, could help others. A seventh grader and a third grader had provided the answer to a question so agonizing that Ron and I could barely comprehend it ourselves. I was proud of them for that.

Ron had learned, through the Wisconsin Donor Network, that both the donor family and the organ recipient could agree to waive confidentiality after one year. It wasn't long before Ron began investigating the legal requirements and completing the necessary paperwork to make that happen.

After Laura's death, Ron and I were surprised by Sara and Rachel's resilience—they rarely broke down or acted out. Even still, we wanted them to know how much we supported them. We tried to avoid putting Laura on a pedestal, and we talked, and even joked, about her in order to give Sara and Rachel unspoken permission to do the same. We were also more transparent than I would've expected about our own emotions and about any after-the-fact medical information we learned. The girls demanded our honesty, and the few times they thought we were trying to hide something, they insisted we not keep secrets from them. We owed them that much.

Much like Ron, Sara needed to keep busy to manage her grief; seventh-grade homework, tennis tournaments, and hanging out with her friends all provided distractions. Ron and I were thankful for the support her friends and classmates provided. Two of her friends, Emily and Michelle—with the help of their middle-school art teacher and a group of other students—created a two-foot-high paper-mache sculpture in memory of Laura. They called their artwork a "beastie," and it was evident how much love they'd poured into this pink, whimsical, animal-like creation. And, with the help of several parents, Sara's seventh-grade class created a large, ceramic plate with the words, *We Love You*, in the center. The border was made of colored thumbprints—one from each of her classmates. Sara didn't talk much when she showed me the platter, but she was deeply touched and her smile said it all. Her friends' support proved more helpful to her than the few therapy sessions she'd attended with Laurie.

Laurie had warned me that because Rachel was only nine years old, she might not understand the true finality of death. I could tell Rachel was trying to work through all that had happened and how it affected her, but most afternoons, she came home and played with her Polly Pocket dolls or Webkinz stuffed animals. For the most part, Rachel kept her feelings about Laura's death to herself, with the exception of her frequent requests for hugs from me. Sometimes our cuddles were for her, but sometimes, I think, they were for me—she often wanted hugs when she sensed I was upset, especially after overhearing my unguarded phone conversations. One afternoon, Rachel told me how she was coping: "I'm going to pretend that Laura's away at college, but that I can't talk with her because the Internet isn't working."

Ron had taken Rachel to one session with Laurie, and although I'd encouraged her to continue, she showed little interest. "Mom, why should I talk to a stranger when I can just talk to you?" she asked. How could I argue? I didn't want to make her feel "broken" in any way. We listened to what Rachel wanted and told her we weren't going to force her to see Laurie, but we stressed that the option was always open.

When the girls first went back to school after Laura's funeral, I'd been concerned about their emotional health. I'd set up meetings with the principals and counselors at both their schools, and we'd crafted plans in case either of them became too upset or overwhelmed during the day. I don't remember if either ever took advantage of the option, but I believe they both took comfort in knowing they could, if they needed to, escape from the classroom. And I did as well.

Sara and Rachel wanted more than anything to be treated normally by their friends and teachers, but at the same time they wanted their sorrow to be respected and acknowledged. Yet many of their classmates didn't understand their loss or know how to talk about it with them. Their teachers, to my surprise, were also inexperienced at expressing their condolences and were similarly unaware of how routine classroom discussions could produce deeply painful moments. For example, Sara came home in tears one afternoon after her French teacher had asked each student to say out loud how many siblings they had. Sara simply didn't know how to respond to these awkward situations, and neither did Rachel. Both felt as if they were being disloyal if they excluded Laura, because "Laura's still our sister."

Rachel has since told me how she recalls little from the second half of that school year. What sticks out in her mind is how some of the other students felt she was getting too much extra attention. I remember that too. One afternoon she told me, "My friend thought she deserved more attention than me because her grandma died. I mean, a grandma dying isn't the same as a sister."

As parents, there was only so much we could do to improve our daughters' experiences at school, yet it was up to us to give them what they truly needed and deserved—stability. Ron and I could only provide that by focusing on their needs, not by being consumed by our own grief. If Ron and I were okay, they would be okay. Losing Laura was our whole family's tragedy to endure, but our lives were ours to reclaim: the choice was ours to make. Ron and I clung tightly to this belief in all we did.

CHAPTER 9

Rewriting the Rules

Spring – Summer 2009

Each time I ventured outside the house, I was unsure of when an unexpected reminder of Laura would strip away my veneer of forced hopefulness. Sometimes, I could make it through the entire day in the new normal, but other days, when a memory would jump out at me, the only way for me to regain my equilibrium was to talk. I did so unapologetically and to anyone who would listen—including strangers. Talking about Laura and retelling her final days quieted the turmoil that never quite left my brain, even on my best days. Talking helped to give me purpose, it was my way of convincing myself that we'd truly done nothing wrong. We were blameless in Laura's death, so if talking about grief's ugliness helped me cope, why shouldn't I?

One afternoon, as a clerk bagged my items at the grocery store, he asked if I had any "fun plans for the weekend." A familiar heaviness compressed my lungs. "Not really," I answered. I paused, looked up at the ceiling, and then directly at him. "A few weeks ago, my fourteen-year-old daughter died suddenly from a brain tumor." His eyes widened; before he could respond, I dived into explaining the brutal events while hoping another customer wouldn't appear behind me and interrupt my therapeutic monologue. I didn't care if I caught him off guard, or if my words disturbed him; maybe that night he would hug his wife or child a little tighter.

On another occasion, while waiting to pick up Sara at her tennis lesson, I was chatting with another mom. When she asked me, innocently enough, how many children I had, I barely hesitated before the words tumbled from my mouth, "Three daughters, a third grader and a seventh grader. And our oldest daughter was a freshman in high school, but she passed away earlier this year." Her cheeks reddened. "Oh, my God, I'm so sorry," she replied. "Did she have other health issues?"

I answered her question with a startling directness. "Laura was a healthy kid. Before this happened, she'd never spent a single day in the hospital." I could sense this mom's understandable desire to distance herself from our reality. I could see her trying to convince herself that her family was different from ours, that her loved ones would always be safe. The woman listened intently as I continued. I didn't change the subject, and she didn't seem to want me to. Knowing full well how disconcerting my words sounded, I still ended our conversation with, "One day can be good, and the next day not so much." I couldn't—wouldn't—whitewash the truth. The unspeakable needed to be spoken.

When I dropped these emotional bombs on relative strangers, I was defying social norms and relying on my gut, and I didn't care if I crossed social boundaries. I was creating my own, more flexible rules to navigate the irrational universe I now inhabited. I now cared less about what was "expected" and was more focused on what would get us through each day.

Sara and Rachel would sometimes complain about how often I would "go there" and share our family's story. I understood their annoyance but couldn't, and didn't want to, stop. Especially on my bad days, I felt addicted to people, to having someone listen. The more people I could tell, the more I felt Laura was still with me.

I'm grateful that most of my friends listened without judging or giving unsolicited advice. They didn't pity or patronize us. (In fact, most commented on how well we seemed to be coping.) Pity would have widened the gap between us. My friends' empathetic behavior conveyed, "I'm here *with* you," not, "I'm here *for* you," and many of them arrived at our door without caring if our kitchen was clean or if I was still in my pajamas. For the first two months, friends also spent countless hours coordinating and preparing meals, which they left in a cooler at our back door. (In the beginning, the girls enjoyed the variety of meals, but, as the weeks passed, they began pleading with me to start cooking again.) I especially appreciated when friends would call from the drugstore or supermarket to ask if they could pick something up for us, which made it easy for me to ask for a few items without feeling as if I were inconveniencing them.

One early show of support, one that Ron and I will never forget, came from the JCC's executive director. He told Ron that he wanted to help us in any way possible. Ron didn't know what to say, and an awkward silence followed. The director then offered a few choices for how he could extend his support. With some hesitancy, Ron agreed to having a massage therapist (from the JCC's health center) come to our home. A massage seemed frivolous, and maybe even disrespectful, so soon after Laura's death, but since norms no longer seemed relevant, we accepted. To this day, we appreciate his unconventional, yet specific, offer; it relieved us of the burden of trying to figure out what we needed.

I was similarly grateful when our neighbor rang our doorbell one afternoon with an unexpected memorial gift. As I opened the door, she pointed to a small crab apple tree on the back of her gardener's truck and asked where we'd like it planted. The tree still stands next to our patio, and each year we look forward to the spring day when its bright pink flowers first bloom.

To Ron and me, these acts of kindness were an unexpected, albeit welcome, type of divine intervention. Initially, we tried to keep track of everyone who offered their help or made contributions to Laura's memorial fund, but it was almost impossible to keep track, and our scribbled list of names soon grew to cover both sides of three spiral-notebook pages. I'd wanted to send every single person an individualized thank-you note, but after writing about twenty handwritten cards, I became overwhelmed by this seemingly never-ending task. My mother and mother-in-law offered to help write them, but even the idea of coordinating their efforts exhausted me. I knew our family and friends would understand; they had offered us their support because we *needed* their support. No one had reached out just so they could receive a thank-you card. I needed to conserve my limited energy for my family—etiquette be damned.

Wherever I went, I was asked about my emotional well-being. I appreciated that, but the often-asked question, "How are you doing?" challenged and frustrated me. If I answered, "Great," I sounded phony and disrespectful to Laura's memory. But if I said, "Horrible," the conversation turned awkward and my family and I would be perceived as victims. Lumping my fluctuating and complicated moods into one all-encompassing adjective was simply not possible; the question, however well intended, resulted in an incredible amount of stress. I preferred the more precisely worded, "How are you doing *today?*" which allowed me to explain that I'd had a nice breakfast with Ron, or that I'd been in a funk in the afternoon and had taken a nap. By having something specific to focus on, I could share what was really on my mind and a genuine conversation could occur.

On many of my "down" afternoons, sadness permeated my cells and I wanted to peel off my skin to relieve the anguish. Sometimes I would walk alone in a nearby nature preserve, where I could talk to Laura aloud: "Please come back. I love you. I miss you." Her body was buried in the ground, but I spoke to the clouds. More often, though, I would call Margie, or another friend, and ask her to walk with me; the lump in my throat would dissipate a few minutes into these on-demand therapy sessions. Being around people helped ease the pain when nothing else would.

I gave myself permission to ask for what I needed. If I reached out to a friend who was busy, I didn't want her to feel guilty. "Don't worry. I'll call someone else," I would say. I wanted to be able to contact her in the future without feeling like I was imposing, because talking proved more effective than sleep, exercise, or writing. Sometimes I would pause mid-sentence and apologize for talking so much, but my friends' reactions would almost always be the same: "It's all right. I want to hear more." My friends supported me and helped me heal, yet I like to think I gave them something too; perhaps they began thinking differently and more deeply about their own lives, without ever having to suffer through a trauma so great themselves.

In these talks, and in my sessions with Laurie, I vented my emotions to a degree few people expected. I crafted my story in order to construct a bearable future. I compartmentalized; I convinced myself that Laura was in a good place, without pain, and that her soul would live on. I was terrified of hearing anything that might challenge this belief. The days surrounding Laura's death were seared into my memory, and I held them sacred. To this day, even though I'm aware my memories are likely flawed, I still become unsettled if someone questions my established version.

I know that friends were sometimes at a loss about what to say. "I'm sorry," or "I'm here for you," was enough. So was a hug. Or flowers. Or an email. Or anything that kept us connected while acknowledging my grief. I didn't want my friends walking on eggshells, ignoring our loss, or editing Laura out of their conversations. I was still Laura's mom, still proud of who she was and what she'd accomplished. I didn't want Laura's friends, their parents, and our friends and family to avoid bringing her up for fear of making me sad. They didn't need to be afraid of mentioning her, since every hour of every day—on both calm days and chaotic ones—some part of me was already thinking about Laura in some way.

I sensed others' relief when I lowered my emotional bar and made myself vulnerable. In exchange for my telling my story, my friends told me theirs. "My story can't compare to losing a child, but . . ." they would begin before sharing their own challenges—medical issues, job losses, marital strife, or financial difficulties. Our exchanges sometimes reminded me of a folktale my mother once told me: "If everyone hung their troubles on a clothesline in the town square, in the end, they would each take back their own problems. The unknown is always scarier than what we're used to dealing with." Listening helped me understand just how universal human suffering truly is.

Comparing suffering and healing seems to be a fundamental part of human behavior, but in my "before life" I hadn't known how to offer condolences to those in mourning. I'd been sheltered as a child from illness and death, except for the funerals of my grandparents and their siblings. When I learned of someone who was facing a loss, a part of me always wanted to take away their sadness, but since I couldn't, I instead ignored their grief. I convinced myself that saying nothing was preferable to saying the wrong thing. Like so many in our culture, I'd never learned to say, "I'm sorry for your loss," or "I'm here if you want to talk." I'm thankful that so many of my friends knew how to do better for me.

Saturdays were my lowest day each week. I'm not sure if this was because Laura was declared brain dead on a Saturday, or if it was simply more difficult for me to pretend that she was at school during the weekends. Whatever the reason, Saturdays were when I missed the five of us being together the most. I felt tormented by the normalcy of our weekends—watching Sara's tennis matches, running errands, attending volunteer events with Ron, or surfing the web on our laptops. All this, and so much more, all resembled our "before life" but with one huge, overwhelming exception: no Laura.

On one particularly suffocating Saturday, I remember waiting anxiously for Ron or the girls to say something—anything at all—about Laura. In a claustrophobic panic, I confronted all three of them and cried, "Don't you guys miss Laura?!" Chaos exploded. "I can't believe you're asking that!" "What's wrong with you?!" "You're being so rude!" they yelled. My offensive words boomeranged in my ears as I realized what I'd just done. "I'm sorry!" I cried, fleeing in tears. Of course they missed Laura: What kind of person asks such an insensitive question? Who was I to dictate how they expressed their sorrow? Their justified outrage shook me to my core: I wasn't acting like the in-control mom I wanted to be. I jumped into my minivan and fled, sobbing as I drove north, with no idea of where I was headed. As I drove, I brushed away my tears with the back of my hand, but I couldn't wipe away the stickiness of grief.

While I continued to have days when I felt utterly miserable, I also had short periods when I (somewhat guiltily) felt like I was myself again. On my forty-third birthday, Ron took me out to dinner. I'd been hesitant; it seemed soon to celebrate any occasion, but Ron convinced me that we deserved to take some time for ourselves. After the waiter brought our entrees, we discussed how oblivious we were to Laura's illness when we'd celebrated Ron's own birthday in early February. A silence fell over us. I thought about Ron's typical communication style: once we'd discussed a topic and agreed on a course of action, he didn't like to revisit it. I wondered if he'd become frustrated if—in the months and years to come—I kept talking about losing Laura. Almost without realizing it, I suddenly asked, "Are you going to be upset if I keep bringing up Laura or what's happened?" Ron looked down at the table and then, with a tear in his eye, he met my gaze. "We can both talk about Laura as much as we want," he replied. "For the rest of our lives. She'll always be part of us."

In the wake of Laura's death, we relaxed our parenting style. We let the girls swear. We were more lenient about their spending money. When I pestered them to clean up their rooms, they responded, "Mom, it's really not that important in the scheme of things," which was hard to argue with. When we were caught in a long traffic jam, when a cell phone broke, or when some other everyday annoyance cropped up, we reminded each other to put it in perspective. More than ever before, we now knew how insignificant these daily frustrations were in the bigger picture.

Yet oddly enough, these frustrations sometimes provoked unexpectedly intense reactions. To help Rachel cope with her sadness, we decided to buy her a pet—something we never would've done if Laura were alive since she was often skittish around animals. In the past, when Sara or Rachel had pleaded for a cat or dog, we'd always said "no" and blamed our decision, for the most part, on Ron's allergies. But when Rachel told us she wanted a pet rat—which her friend Morgan said was "the new hamster"—we caved.

At the pet store, Rachel thankfully liked the white, furry rats much more than the hairless, red-eyed ones. She picked out her two favorites, along with an exercise wheel, cage, and food. On the drive home, we joked about how Laura, being somewhat germ-phobic, would've been less than thrilled about our new houseguests.

On the following day, which was a day off of school, Rachel asked if she could let the smaller rat run around on the kitchen floor, just like Morgan did with hers. I hesitated, but again I caved. Seconds later, we watched as the rat scurried along the baseboard, then disappeared into the crevice underneath the dishwasher. Rachel burst into tears and blamed herself. "I can't lose the first pet I've ever had," she cried. "I lost my sister, I can't lose my rat, too!" I comforted her as best I could. As crazy as it sounds, the rat's escape felt like another loss, another shock to our system—it triggered a surge of emotion in both of us that I never could've anticipated. Rachel and I alternated between crying over the disappearance and laughing at our stupidity: How dumb was it to let a rat run freely around the kitchen? How did losing a rodent feel so awful? How were we this vulnerable? Did we really deserve this level of aggravation?

At any other time in our lives, I probably wouldn't have

expected Ron to help until he came home from work, but now I called him at his office. Whereas the "before Ron" likely wouldn't have left work in the middle of the day (except in a true emergency), when he heard the hysteria in my voice, he came home almost immediately. Still in his suit, Ron made a peanut butter trap and placed it underneath the sink. After two hours of lying on his stomach and watching the trap, he achieved hero status with a live capture.

Our parenting styles also changed in other, more surprising, ways. Despite my ongoing panic about Sara and Rachel's health, we decided not to schedule MRIs for them (or for ourselves), although many parents of Laura's classmates had done just that. Since Laura's cancer wasn't genetic, we needed to take that leap of faith, to believe that the unthinkable wouldn't repeat itself. While Sara initially had some interest in getting "a full-body MRI," Rachel did not, and Ron and I decided these tests would add more stress to our already too-tenuous sense of safety. We tried as much as we could to let go of the many "what ifs" and instead concentrate on what felt right for our family.

What felt right for our family, though, had shifted—as had our family dynamic. Sara was thrust into the oldest-child role, and although Rachel was still the youngest, she now had only one sister to look up to, to learn from, and to have fun with. And, now that we had only two living daughters, the time and attention that we'd devoted to Laura could be lavished on Sara and Rachel. Yet, we would always be the parents of three daughters, with love and energy enough for all of them: losing Laura couldn't ever change that.

When, early in our marriage, Ron and I discussed having children, we had purposefully decided on three—most likely because we'd both been raised in three-child families. We were willing to be "outnumbered by our kids" because we thought there would be less competitiveness between siblings if they were a trio. Now we were back to one parent per child, although sibling rivalry was no longer a worry. With Laura gone, Sara and Rachel could no longer take their relationship for granted, and they became more tightly bonded than ever before. If Sara lost a tennis match, Rachel would now make it a point to console her and give her a hug; if Rachel needed help with her math homework, Sara would offer to explain any confusing word problems. They called themselves "besties." They would both become annoyed when their friends complained about or under-appreciated their siblings. They understood the magnitude of all they'd lost, and they vowed openly to appreciate each other more. And they have. To this day, they remain closer, I believe, than most sisters.

Susan and Ron, senior year in high school—1983

Rachel, Laura, Ron, Susan, and Sara—Fall 2003

Laura's class picture, 2008—eighth grade

Miller family holiday photo—2008

Ron and Laura—Israel, December 2008

#87
Miranda

#98
Hanna

Laura's memorial display case at Nicolet High School on
dedication day—October 2011. Dress designs by Laura Miller.

Ron, Susan, Sara, and Rachel Miller; Trish and Gary O'Neill
—Milwaukee, September 2012

Rachel, Susan, Ron, and Sara at Rachel's *bat mitzvah*
—November 2012

CHAPTER 10

Channeling Pain into Action

When Ron became a father, he embraced fatherhood in a way that initially surprised me: he was a more modern, hands-on dad than mine had been. He cherished his relationship with each of our daughters, and when he returned home from his long workdays (often after the four of us had already eaten dinner), all three girls frequently greeted him with "running hugs." Beyond the hugs and kisses, Ron also made it a point to tell them each day that he loved them. His parenting was different from the experiences of my childhood: in my family, I knew in my heart that we all loved each other, but we didn't express that love so effusively. I also remember him calling each of the girls by their made-up nicknames—"Laura-Bora," "Sara-Beara," and "Ray-Ray"—more often than I did. Ron helped me become more outwardly affectionate and lighthearted, yet I still somehow got stuck being the "bad cop" on the rare occasions when one of our daughters acted out.

In the early years, when our family was still growing, Ron was asked if he liked being a dad. He often replied with a grin, "There's nothing better than watching a football game with a baby asleep on my lap and a beer in my hand." Each time I was pregnant, when friends or family asked him if he wanted a son, Ron often said, "It doesn't matter whether it's a boy or a girl, as long as we bring home a healthy baby from the hospital."

Almost literally, Ron wanted to give our daughters the world. When Laura was in the first grade, we started taking the whole family on overseas trips during winter and spring school breaks. We made it a point to visit cities and historical sites rather than beaches and all-inclusive resorts. On every trip, Ron's job was to steer our always-overstacked luggage cart while I pushed Rachel in the stroller; Laura and Sara usually walked between us. Other travelers often looked with empathy at our loaded-down caravans, but all these trips were worth the effort. They provided shared memories and bonding time for the five of us, and Ron and I believed these adventures were invaluable learning experiences. Taking long overseas flights, waiting during unexpected delays, and dealing with all the other hassles of travel taught all of us patience and flexibility, just as our travels exposed the girls to history and culture far beyond what they could ever learn in school.

Rows of framed photographs from our trips still hang in the finished area of our basement. The most unusual framed remembrance, though, isn't a personal photo, but a newspaper clipping. On our trip to Madrid in December of 2006, the parking garage connected to the airport was bombed minutes before our taxi driver dropped us off for our return flight. After waiting six hours with the throngs of other confused and delayed travelers, we were unable to reach our gate and had to spend an extra night in Spain. Before finding another flight home the next day, Ron picked up a local newspaper to remember the incident, but it wasn't until several weeks later that Laura—who was trying to strengthen her seventh-grade Spanish skills—found a picture of our family sitting on the airport floor; there we were, prominently displayed on page three, surrounded by our luggage. We didn't know we'd been photographed, and Ron still jokes about how it's usually "not a good sign" to be featured in a local newspaper when traveling.

When Ron went back to the office after Laura's funeral, he received less emotional support at work than I did. Although all of them had come to the funeral or *shiva*, his colleagues and coworkers shied away from personal conversations while in the office. He knew they cared, but he also knew that they feared breaching the line between the professional and the personal. More often than not, the empathy he did receive came from the female support staff. In the male-leadership-dominated world of investment banking, the women were more willing to articulate their care and concern. They were the ones who would check up on him and ask how our family was doing. They were the ones who knew, when they heard the quiver in my voice on the phone, that they needed to find Ron immediately, even if it meant interrupting an internal meeting.

In our society, men are generally discouraged from showing the complicated emotions of grief, which is why I believe Ron channeled so much of his pain into action, rather than into words or tears. Whereas I, as a grieving mom, could cry, or complain, or talk as much as I needed to, Ron had to manage his grief while also conforming to a more rigid set of expectations. For me, I also had the luxury of returning to my volunteer work on my own terms—and I could choose how much or how little I wanted to take on—but Ron didn't have the same freedom. As a senior member of his firm, an extended leave of absence wouldn't have been viable (or even desirable) for him. Fair or not, his job, and our livelihood, depended on Ron's managing his work and his sorrow simultaneously—a feat I'm still unsure how he managed.

Staying at home longer might have given him a few weeks of private mourning, but the stress of *not* being at work would most likely have been worse for him.

Laura's death in February of 2009 coincided with the height of the financial crisis, which followed the fall 2008 stock market crash. At any other point in his career, Ron would've been seriously troubled by the decline in his firm's revenue, but now all events paled in comparison to losing Laura: he focused on our family first, all else became a distant second. When one of his deals fell apart or his firm lost yet another financially struggling client, Ron no longer let it upset him. "It's not worth losing sleep over," he'd say. He also became inherently bolder and began confronting workplace challenges head-on—before they became real problems—without worrying so much about stepping on toes. With Laura gone, "the worst" had already happened in his life; what was there now to be so afraid of?

Ron's management style also changed in the wake of his grief. He became more sensitive to his colleagues' struggles. Laura's death helped him to understand—more powerfully than ever before—that his team shows up to work each day not only as employees, but as individuals with family responsibilities, health challenges, and worries. He also learned the importance of focusing on his clients' personal goals as much as on their financial projections. I remember many evenings when he told me about his increased efforts to balance both.

As he grew emotionally, Ron also became less afraid of having difficult conversations. He became more comfortable reaching out to colleagues who were facing illness or the death of a loved one. Since our family had received so much generous support from such a wide circle of friends, Ron and I now feel compelled to do the same for others: confronting the uncomfortable no longer feels like a choice, but a basic responsibility.

Even with Ron's new sensitivities, meeting new clients still proved challenging for him; the usual small talk often included the question, "How many children do you have?" If he answered, "three kids," he'd have to brace himself for the awkward follow-up questions about their ages and interests. If he answered, "two kids," he wasn't being true to himself or honest about our family, but this simpler response kept the meeting focused and professional. "It's hard either way," he once confessed, "because I don't want to hide something that's so important to who I am." It's something he still struggles with, even now. To this day, he keeps a framed photo of all three girls on his desk, and he uses an old family photo of the five of us as his smartphone's screensaver. He wants to make sure each of his coworkers knows him on both a personal and professional level.

Business-related social events also came with challenges. Especially in the early years, Ron and I felt as if all eyes were on us; like a magnet, we attracted some people but repelled others. When we talked about losing Laura at these gatherings, we sensed the fear we struck into many parents' hearts. Those who had experienced hardships in their own lives were more likely to approach us with confidence, pierce through social niceties, and "go deep" with us quickly. We appreciated their willingness to grapple with our trauma; being able to discuss in a social setting the one subject that mattered most to us—Laura and our ongoing grief—created deeper relationships and transformed acquaintances into friends.

While these cocktail-type events were initially difficult for us both, they no longer intimidate Ron or me. When we scan a roomful of guests, we now recognize that each person, regardless of how well-put-together they appear, harbors their own challenges and worries—so why should we be intimidated? Although the loss of our child was more public than most adversities, we understand we're not alone in being vulnerable—we're all bound by fears, sorrows, and death's inevitability. Knowing we share this basic human reality makes these connections more genuine and meaningful.

One of the unexpected consequences of losing Laura was the underlying assumption that our marriage would be in jeopardy. When friends were genuine and brave enough to ask us "how we were doing," Ron and I detected their undertone: was our marriage still strong, or were we at risk for divorce? Their concern, I learned, stemmed from a surprisingly common misconception—popularized by Harriet Sarnoff Schiff's 1974 book, *The Bereaved Parent*—that asserts that couples experience serious marital difficulties after the death of a child.

In her book, Schiff claimed that up to ninety percent of bereaved couples will face potentially-marriage-ending difficulties, but the reality, I believe, is far more complex. A child's death can build or destroy any relationship, and much depends on that relationship's health prior to the trauma—as well as on how the couple chooses to react to their loss. (Far more modern studies, too, have debunked Schiff's claims: a 2006 survey commissioned by The Compassionate Friends, a bereavement organization, found that the divorce rate among parents facing child loss was only sixteen percent.) Even in the midst of the unthinkable, Ron and I didn't lash out at each other or blame one another. Since neither of us, mercifully, was responsible for Laura's cancer, there was no guilt or blame to assign. We understood, without much discussion, that above all else our combined energy was essential for parenting Sara and Rachel, and we became a team in a whole new way. Today, after thirty years of marriage, Ron and I still bicker about the little things (I'm embarrassed to admit that I'm often the one who initiates these squabbles), but we very rarely argue about the truly essential issues that could undermine our marriage.

When I consider how I endured losing Laura, I attribute my survival to Ron. He channeled much of his seemingly limitless energy into everyday household tasks, which meant I had more energy to give Sara and Rachel as they learned how to live in our new normal. He somehow managed to temper the turmoil as we moved forward in our marriage—and as a family.

Although Ron didn't express his sadness at the same times or in the same ways as I did, I sensed that he often grieved through me, and through our daily conversations about Laura: as her parents, we knew it would always be impossible for anyone else to understand the loss of someone so central to our existence. Ron and I knew the hole in our hearts would stay with us forever, yet through our shared heartache we somehow forged an even stronger, more-exclusive connection between us. That bond gave us a better chance at reclaiming our lives, a way of focusing on all that was still possible for ourselves and our family.

CHAPTER 11

Shattering Illusions

Spring – Summer 2009

L aura, you look so good in those jeans," I said with a cautious optimism as she stepped out of the dressing room. Laura examined herself in the three-way mirror, but she didn't reply or meet my gaze. I knew what was bothering her. She wanted the Seven for All Mankind jeans to fit more snugly on her slim frame, to hug her backside more tightly. This was Laura's personal fashion dilemma: if the pant length worked, the waist was too wide; if the waistline fit, the legs were too short. I looked forward to the day when we'd find her the perfect pair of jeans and she'd come out of the dressing room with a smile.

I snapped out of my memory-daydream just as the mom in the minivan parked in front of me applied her lipstick. As I sat in the school pick-up line waiting for Sara, I imagined this mom's most pressing problem was what to make for dinner that evening. I ached for my "before life" of ordinary, everyday concerns.

I opened the car window and breathed in the warm spring air. Usually, spring's arrival delighted me, but this year the signs of renewal seemed to mock me. Functioning in the new normal, while also putting on a brave-as-possible face for Sara and Rachel, made me feel as though I was still in the depths of winter while the rest of the world moved onward. Routine tasks—making lunches, signing permission slips, driving to after-school activities—now exhausted me. Months of managing my widely fluctuating emotions had sapped my usual hopefulness and positivity. My optimism hadn't just vanished, it seemed to have taken a chunk of me with it. The world now felt distant somehow, blurry.

I focused my gaze on the afternoon sun. As it disappeared behind a massive gray cloud, a startling clarity pierced through my hazy thoughts without warning, almost as if I'd broken out of a spell. The idea of a logical and compassionate universe suddenly fell away. I'd built my entire existence on the concept of life "owing" me certain basic things, but now I saw just how flawed that assumption was. Truly, I was entitled to nothing. Nothing had guaranteed my finding a husband. Nothing had guaranteed my being able to have children. Nothing had guaranteed my being born in America. For the most part, these advantages—and so many more—were accidents of circumstance. Our family's trauma was an arbitrary and minuscule tragedy within an immense and likely random cosmos. None of us were guaranteed happiness or a certain lifespan, none of us entitled to a long, healthy life. How arrogant I had been to presume otherwise! Instead of questioning, "Why us?" I should've been asking, "Why *not* us?"

I saw our loss for what it was—one heartache among millions, maybe billions, of others. We would have to deal with our sorrow just like so many countless others had done in the past and would do in the years to come. No omnipotent hand dictated my fate, controlled my life, or puppeteered me as if I were a marionette. Blaming God, seething in resentment, or even losing faith in our religion would be just as pointless as castigating anyone or anything else. Perhaps Laura died because she'd already accomplished her destiny; perhaps her death was a fluke of nature in a universe that simply was not—and would never be—fair. There was no way of knowing. In that moment, something entirely new came to me: Laura's death didn't signify the end of the world, just the end of the world I had known.

I jumped as Sara opened the car door. My introspection faded as she told me about her day at school, just as she did every afternoon. Yet something in me had shifted. With the last of my idealistic expectations wiped away, I could now let go of the "what ifs" and acknowledge the "what is." No personal misfortune— not mine or anyone else's—would stop the world from turning, and I would have to forgive the cosmos for not delivering on a guarantee it never offered in the first place.

My newfound insight continued to shape my thoughts, creating small epiphanies in the everyday. I started becoming more genuinely grateful for what my family and I still had, rather than forcing myself, with little conviction, to count my blessings. Yet doubts and fears still swirled inside me, creating a paradox of sorts. Being genuinely grateful didn't mean I wasn't also in dread of another crisis, especially not in a universe I now knew to be devoid of guarantees.

One evening, when Sara complained of a headache, my heart skipped a beat and a silent scream lodged in my throat. I fumbled to our medicine cabinet. I handed her a glass of water and a Tylenol as I remembered the many times I'd done the same for Laura. As soon as Sara went back into the den where she couldn't see me, I sat down to steady myself. My pulse pounded in my ears, and my breathing quickened. "Stay calm," I told myself. "Don't panic. Don't show the girls your fear."

I ran upstairs to find Ron. "Susan, relax. Sara will be fine," he assured me as best he could. "It's just a headache," he said calmly.

I exploded. "How do you know it's *just* that? You weren't the one who cared for Laura when she was in pain! You weren't at home when she had the seizure!" Ron didn't respond. I'm certain the "before Ron" would've teased me about being a little bit neurotic, but now he gave me his full attention. He listened to my fears, although he couldn't take them away.

Before she went to bed a few hours later, Sara complained that her head still hurt. My nervous system again switched into overdrive. A primal fear choked both my logic and my lungs: Did I need to call an ambulance? How could I keep her safe? I tried to calm myself, tried to remind myself that most headaches are temporary, treatable, and are caused by something minor, like stress or hormones. Reasoning with myself didn't work; I spent half the night frozen in fear.

Sara felt fine, thankfully, the next morning, but a few weeks later, when she suffered from another headache, we surrendered to our anxiety—and hers—and scheduled an MRI. Waiting for the results was terrifying, but hearing the doctor's reassuring words was worth it. Yet I knew our fears were only temporarily alleviated, because MRI scans only capture the current point in time. The future, as always, would remain an uncertainty we all would have to deal with, Sara and Rachel included.

Fielding questions about Laura's death was similarly unsettling—my nerves often kicked into high gear when I had to answer them. Even though these questions were well-intentioned, the remarks only served to compound our vulnerability. Ron and I never knew when we'd be asked:

"Do you live near power lines?"
"Maybe too much cell phone use caused Laura's tumor?"
"How do you know the tumor wasn't genetic? Should Sara and Rachel be tested?"

The blame embedded in these questions upset us, because the implication was that if we'd done something differently, Laura would still be alive. Neither of us could cope with believing that we had somehow, contributed to the loss of our daughter.

As the school year ended, I kept myself busy planning Sara's rescheduled *bat mitzvah* party, which we would be holding in mid-June. Ron and I had questioned whether it was appropriate to host such a major celebration only four months after burying Laura, but we agreed that celebrating Sara's becoming a *bat mitzvah* far outweighed whatever norms we were expected to follow; Sara deserved a traditional party just like we'd originally planned. Who said we had to do anything "by the book" if it wasn't right for our family?

As the date approached, Ron and I mentally prepared ourselves for what we knew would be the surreal task of receiving condolences alongside congratulations. We'd firmly decided, though, that Sara deserved a happy day, and we were committed to making that happen. If we needed to console our guests even as we celebrated Sara, so be it. We would have to embrace all our emotions, joy included.

The night of the party arrived. Throughout the evening, which was festive and upbeat, I thought about Laura—as I'm sure many others did—but I was also able to enjoy myself. Without much urging from the DJ, friends and family joined us on the dance floor before dinner; I was surprised by my being able to let go and immerse myself in the music. Minutes later, after we'd caught our breath from dancing the *hora*, Ron and I formally welcomed our guests and recited the *shehecheyanu*, my favorite prayer. (The *shehecheyanu* thanks God for allowing us to come together and celebrate on this day.) After dinner, but before dessert, Sara and her friends gathered in front of a large projection screen, while the adults stood behind them. Ron had spent dozens of hours creating a video montage for Sara's originally planned *bat mitzvah* party, and he'd recently re-edited it to include footage from her rescheduled service. The lights dimmed as images of Laura, Sara, and Rachel—from birthday parties, family gatherings, and vacations—flashed on the screen. As the video played, I found myself alone at the back of the room, reliving the memories. I hugged myself and blinked back bittersweet tears.

Two weeks later, with the summer in full swing, Sara and Rachel left for their (respective) summer trips—we'd arranged these plans for them in the fall, just as we did every year. Sara was flying to Oregon for a three-week hiking-and-rock-climbing group trip, and Rachel was off to a two-week overnight camp an hour away from home.

The week before, I'd debated with Ron if we should let them go. He'd replied quickly. "Susan, we already signed them up. It'll be a good distraction. They need to go on with their lives." He was right of course, and I knew we couldn't bubble-wrap them: I wanted Sara and Rachel to live their own lives, more now than ever before. After all, Laura had been a cautious child—she'd followed the rules and done everything right—but that still hadn't prevented her cancer. So why shouldn't we let our surviving daughters travel and go to camp? If we didn't let them go as planned, we'd be teaching them to live in fear of the "next bad thing," rather than embracing the good times.

From Milwaukee, we followed Sara's itinerary and looked forward to her calling when her group emerged from the backcountry. I became agitated when we didn't hear from her on the scheduled day, and I panicked when I read about bear attacks in Oregon on the Internet. "Susan, bad news travels fast," Ron reassured me, but even his resolve wavered when we called the camp's main office and were repeatedly greeted by a voicemail prompt.

Ron soon realized that Sara almost certainly would've bought something if her group had made it out of the wilderness safely. We logged into our bank account online to check for activity on Sara's debit card. It was a genius idea—Sara had bought a drink in Bend, Oregon, earlier in the day. I pressed my hand to my heart in relief: she was fine! When Sara called us the next morning, she explained that the camp had sent us the itinerary for another group.

It was a tradition in our family to spend a week each summer at Camp Michigania, the camp for University of Michigan alums and their families. During this week, the girls always participated in organized camp activities (with Laura, of course, gravitating to arts and crafts), while Ron and I enjoyed time by ourselves—sailing, horseback riding, or reading on our cabin porch. Along with other families, we ate meals together in the community dining hall, painted pottery, sang silly songs, and ate s'mores around the campfire. Every year, we also looked forward to staying with our longtime cabin mates, a family of five with three daughters. Even without Laura, we chose to continue this much-loved tradition—how could we take anything else away from Sara and Rachel when they'd already lost so much?

The first day of our camp week curiously coincided with Laura's fifteenth birthday, and although we tried coming up with a more creative way to commemorate the day, we settled on releasing balloons. Around dusk, the four of us gathered at the lake, then let our pink balloons go one at a time. When it was my turn, I held my breath as my balloon zigzagged in the breeze, barely missing the branches of a nearby tree. It then hung motionless over the lake for a moment before disappearing into the gray clouds above. Sara and Rachel, perhaps embarrassed by the ritual, seemed uncomfortable and quickly ran off to be with their friends. With the bottom of my T-shirt, I wiped away a few tears, then I grabbed Ron's hand. We returned to our cabin, where we passed around a bowl of chocolate-covered gummy bears—Laura's favorite candy—and listened as our cabin mates shared their favorite memories of her.

CHAPTER 12

Wired to Survive

Fall 2009 – Spring 2010

When Laura was a baby, Ron and I counted the number of months since her birth: now we tallied the months since her death. Each month marked another school or family event without her. When making restaurant reservations, I winced when I asked for a table for four, not five, and, when traveling, I felt a similar prick when we no longer needed to request a cot in our hotel room. As time moved forward, so many minor yet painful reminders stayed with me.

In September, the girls went back to school—Sara to eighth grade and Rachel to fourth—yet Laura would never move on to tenth grade. At our synagogue's *Rosh Hashanah* services that month, I couldn't concentrate on the prayers; instead, I yearned to feel Laura's head on my shoulder, her hand in mine, as she restlessly waited for the service to end, just as she'd done so many times before.

At the beginning of what should have been her sophomore year, Laura's BBYO chapter told us they were organizing a walk in October in Laura's memory; funds would be designated for brain cancer research. I was eager to assist with the planning. To publicize the event (and after hours of painstaking deliberation on my part), we combined Laura's "Lola" fashion signature with a simple, seven-petal flower outline that she'd painted in the summer of 2008. I hoped Laura, wherever she was, approved of the design.

In a local forest preserve, on a sunny Sunday morning, more than one hundred and fifty people joined us at the walk, including our extended family, many of Laura's teachers, and dozens of all three of our daughters' friends. Before the event began, Ron welcomed the participants and thanked them for honoring Laura's life in this thoughtful way. He then pointed to a nearby easel where we'd displayed the thank-you note from the woman who'd received Laura's liver. At the conclusion of his comments, he urged everyone to become an organ donor.

Witnessing so many people coming together—even eight months after Laura's death—reminded me of how strongly our community, and their open hearts, had impacted our healing. The walk's funds were donated to the American Brain Tumor Association. Although Ron and I doubted that medulloblastomas could be prevented or cured, we hoped the contributions might fund medical advances that would help those suffering from other brain tumors.

A few weeks after the memorial walk, while in a coffee shop, I saw a parent of a student in Laura's grade—she pretended to scan a display of mugs to avoid a conversation. In my "before life" I probably would've avoided the uncomfortable interaction, but now I was fearless as I approached her and asked about her daughter. "Oh, she's fine," she responded as her face reddened and her eyes began welling with tears. "She works at the clothing store down the road." "Oh, that was Laura's favorite," I replied. "She loved the jeans there."

I instantly sensed this mom's relief; by intentionally mentioning Laura, I had given this woman permission to talk about her—and to talk to me as "Laura's mom." I didn't want her to think I resented her, or any other parents, for being proud of their children's accomplishments, and I still wanted to remain connected to Laura's world outside of our home. Without Laura to link us to her friends, their parents, and her teachers, I knew some of these relationships would fade organically over time, but I was still Laura's mom and I still had the right to take pride in her achievements.

Like her BBYO chapter, Laura's high school also wanted to honor her in some way. The student council, along with the freshman humanities teachers, reached out to us with initial ideas for a memorial. I was touched by how deeply they still cared and grateful for their enthusiasm for the project. After a few meetings together, we decided to design a display case that would house rotating exhibits of students' fashion designs and other art projects.

Realizing our vision took longer than expected, but the planning sessions gave these students a way to keep connected to Laura—and kept our family connected to them. In the fall of 2011, in what would have been Laura's junior year, Nicolet High School hosted a dedication ceremony. The case's memorial plaque reads, "In celebration of Laura Miller's love of fashion, art, and writing," and the first exhibit showcased four dresses that two students and Rachel (with the help of Laura's sewing teacher) had created from Laura's sketches. I was proud that we'd achieved for Laura her dream of being a fashion designer. At the dedication, Ron and I also announced that, with the help of the contributions to Laura's memorial fund, we'd officially established an annual scholarship in our daughter's name for Nicolet's college-bound seniors.

Even with the generous community remembrances, as time passed (and the periods between my more difficult episodes of grief lengthened), I feared we were forgetting about Laura in some sense. Our early sadness kept her close to us in a palpable way: if we stopped tethering ourselves to the pain, would Laura become a distant memory? Part of me was petrified of letting go of my sorrow or of forgetting any memory of her, no matter how small.

But I was also beginning to accept that less sadness couldn't ever detract from my love. Laura would always be my bright, beautiful daughter, and I only needed to glance at my wrist to remind me of that. I'd found Laura's bracelet, tangled up in my necklaces, a few weeks after the funeral. She'd received the Tiffany bracelet—a substantial silver chain with a heart pendant—as a *bat mitzvah* gift, and it had instantly become her favorite piece of jewelry. When I discovered it, a pang of guilt had caused me to hesitate before fastening the toggle clasp—the bracelet was Laura's, not mine, to wear. Yet in the months that followed, having Laura's bracelet encircling my left wrist grounded me and comforted me.

I've rarely taken it off since. On most days, the bracelet brings pleasant memories of Laura flooding back; on other days, it's tangible proof that she existed, that I didn't conjure up the tragedy, that I'm sane. Several times each day, I jiggle my arm to make sure the bracelet is still there. It's become an extension of my body—my attempt at lessening the phantom ache of her absence.

As winter approached, I believed the worst of the grieving was behind me. I thought I was in control: the sadness, the change in identity, the vulnerability, the confusion, and the loneliness were all still with me, but they were becoming less and less overwhelming. When Laurie, who I hadn't seen in several weeks, called to ask when I'd like to schedule our next appointment, I told her I didn't think it was necessary.

"Susan, you're still in the first year," she responded. "The grief isn't over yet." I was irritated: I didn't understand why she would presume to know the depth or longevity of my grief. I told her I'd check my calendar and call her later, but I put off calling her back. Even though I missed Laura every day, I was tired of seeking "healing strategies" for a problem to which there was no solution. Yet when a fresh wave of grief hit me two weeks later and I plunged into a longer-than-usual low, I reluctantly called Laurie and scheduled a follow-up. I still needed her support and guidance, and I'd still have to be willing to accept her help.

A week or two before *Hanukkah*, as I was flipping through a magazine, a short review for *The Other Side of Sadness: What the New Science of Bereavement Tells Us about Life after Loss* caught my attention. It was the first book I'd found on grieving and healing that looked as if it approached loss from an analysis-based perspective, rather than offering anecdotes and falsely comforting clichés. I bought the book and read it within a day. The author, George A. Bonanno, a clinical psychologist and a grief researcher at Columbia University's Teachers College, studies the experiences of those coping with loss. His research for the book included dozens of case studies in which participants spoke freely about their real, personal experiences with grief—not about what they were "expected" to feel while in mourning.

What Bonanno suggests is that humans, regardless of country or culture, have an intuitive ability to persevere—and even flourish—after heartbreaking losses. Mourners, even those who have suffered through a child's death, can be resilient: they can and do resume their lives. He also believes that because many grieve without seeking counseling, healthy grief experiences are likely underreported, which is a large part of why our views on loss are distorted.

Also according to Bonanno, those who *do* seek therapy should not be viewed as helpless victims with a lifelong condition—and certainly they shouldn't be told to "look on the bright side" when in the first throes of grief. Bonanno says these attitudes are a byproduct of our Western culture, which doesn't deal well with death. Hospitals and nursing homes shield us from the dying process and the inevitability of loss. Violent video games and TV programs desensitize us to, and distance us from, death. We're taught to avoid talking about real-world mourning and grief at all costs, even more so than other taboo topics like money, sex, religion, or politics. In his book, Bonanno advocates for a more honest way of sharing our most painful experiences and emotions—something that was an absolute need for me, especially in those first months.

The Other Side of Sadness validated my own beliefs. Although Ron and I had lost our firstborn, we were not fated or required to be miserable for the rest of our lives. The survivors' stories in Bonanno's book centered on the theory that our DNA is wired to survive loss. Like others who had come before us, our family could choose to be okay, or even better than okay. We didn't need to feel guilty about it, we didn't need to apologize for it. The book affected me so deeply that I asked Ron to read it too, and a week later I gave Laurie a copy as a *Hanukkah* present.

My outlook for our future happiness was becoming more hopeful, but many worries stayed with me. On one of my frequent walks with Margie, I shared the fundamental fear I'd been harboring since the weather turned wintery. "I'm worried that once the first-year anniversary passes, people will think it's been enough time, that I should be done grieving. I'm afraid they'll become tired of listening to me talk about Laura." Margie's response was steeped in compassion. "Susan, your friends will always be there for you, and you can talk to me whenever and for however long you want. There's no magic in the anniversary date."

And she was right. Not only was there no magic, but there was no escaping the flashbacks that became more frequent again after the New Year. Laura's seizure, her four days of unresponsiveness, her *shiva*, and so many other memories assaulted me. I even remembered events I'd suppressed: Laura had once asked me, while in the midst of an especially painful headache, if she had a brain tumor. "I don't want to die," she'd cried as I tried my best to comfort her. "Of course you're not going to die," I'd said reassuringly, never imagining the weeks ahead were possible in any reality.

When a friend asked me how we were planning to observe the February 21st anniversary, I realized that I especially didn't want to be alone on February 18th—the day Laura had stopped breathing and the day I believed she truly died. I invited five close friends—all of whom had weathered the last year with me—to my house for lunch; gathering together provided needed focus for the day, and, as expected, talking with friends made the heaviness much lighter.

As the end of February grew near, friends and family were thinking about Laura too; some sent us cards or posted messages to her Facebook page. Ron, Sara, and Rachel also had Laura close in their thoughts. The four of us marked the anniversary somberly and peacefully as a family. On the evening of February 20th, we lit a *yahrzeit* candle, which burned for twenty-four hours—from sundown to sundown—in honor of Laura.

In the spring, our extended family returned, with our rabbi, to the cemetery for the first time since the burial. Ron had coordinated the arrangements for the headstone-unveiling ceremony, largely shielding me from any planning that would've made me think about Laura's body being in the ground. Ron had already visited the grave twice, but I hadn't accompanied him. Her body was in the cemetery, but that's not where I wanted to remember Laura. I'd given myself permission not to go with him—even if graveside visits were something a grieving mom was "expected" to do.

Even though the warm spring temperatures made the site less ominous, I couldn't erase the image of the vault cover crashing onto Laura's coffin. As the headstone was unveiled, our rabbi recited prayers, including the now-too-familiar *Kaddish*. I hugged Sara and Rachel close. I fixed my eyes on the granite marker, which was engraved with, "Beloved Daughter, Sister, Granddaughter, and Friend." A Star of David was etched above, and below was Laura's seven-petal flower design—a symbol of her youthful and enduring creative spirit.

Part II
Permission to Thrive

CHAPTER 13

Our Miracle

August 2010 & April 2011

I removed an envelope from the Wisconsin Donor Network from our mailbox. My heart skipped a beat as I ripped it open. Today marked exactly eighteen months since Laura had stopped breathing, and something inside me knew that this was the letter we'd been long awaiting. My hands shook as I unfolded the contents. I glanced at the form letter, but it was the next page I was interested in. On a plain white piece of paper, four lines were typed: Patricia Lynn O'Neill's name, street address, city, and phone number. This was the woman who'd received Laura's liver, the woman who we'd been restricted from communicating with directly. Questions swirled in my mind: What would she look like? Would we have anything else in common with her? Would we like her? Would she like us? Would we feel a bond with her? I rushed to the computer in our living room, went online, and searched for information on Patricia Lynn O'Neill. I found links to three women with similar names, but none who lived in New York.

I ran over to my neighbor Heidi's house and elatedly told her the news. I hadn't planned to show Sara the letter until Ron came home from work but, in my excitement, I'd left it in plain view by the computer. By the time I returned home, Sara had succeeded in finding two video clips of a woman in New York named "Trish" O'Neill; knowing she'd found the right person, Sara shouted to me with joy.

We watched the videos together. In the first one, Trish assured her class of young children that she was recovering well and would be back at school soon. The second video was a local news feature; the anchor explained how Trish's liver had been donated by a fourteen-year-old girl. I gasped as I squeezed Sara's shoulders. "Oh, my God. Sara, did you just hear that? This is so crazy!"

That night, we went out to dinner. Ron, Sara, and Rachel talked over each other excitedly and with a passion that none of us had shown in a long time. I tried to focus on their conversation as I internalized what we'd just learned. We'd known that Laura's liver had been successfully matched—that it was inside of someone else's body—but now it felt real. Trish O'Neill. A woman we now could talk to and perhaps even meet. "Let's call her tonight," Sara said with a definitiveness that surprised me. She was leaving the next day for a five-day tennis trip in northern Wisconsin, and I heard the urgency in her voice as she continued, "I don't want to wait to talk to her until I get back. You *can't* make me wait!"

My heart pounded as I began voicing my objections. I wanted more time to organize my thoughts before calling, but Sara, Rachel, and Ron's persistence and curiosity won out. Minutes after we arrived home, Ron picked up the landline in the kitchen and dialed Trish's number. I grabbed another phone and stepped out onto our screened porch. The girls ran upstairs to use another extension. A man answered, and Ron explained who we were. I held my breath.

Within seconds, Trish came on the line. "I'm so glad to be talking to you," she said with tears in her voice. We talked for a while, making introductions and covering the basics. She was nice. Upbeat. Kind. Open. She was married to Gary, an Irish-Catholic man who worked in law enforcement. He was seventeen years her senior, and consequently—even though she was only forty years old—Trish had several young step-grandkids who called her their "grammie." With the skill of a teacher, Trish made sure to include Sara and Rachel in our conversation by asking them about their interests and encouraging them to describe Laura. I was impressed by Trish's sensitivity.

Thirty minutes later, we ended the call with promises to keep in touch. "I can't believe how well that went," I said to Ron as I walked back into the kitchen, hoping he felt the same way. He smiled at me, and as I drew closer to him I saw tears of relief and happiness in his eyes.

Sara and Rachel ran downstairs and started dancing around the kitchen. "Oh, my God, that was so amazing!" Sara cried. "She's so nice!" Rachel shouted. I couldn't remember the last time we'd all been this happy and excited. Talking to Trish had invigorated us in a way that I'd doubted was still possible.

We'd decided to donate Laura's organs on the most traumatic day of our lives. And, because of that decision, Trish was alive. In saving Trish's life, Laura had left a profoundly meaningful and awe-inspiring legacy—one that would've made her beyond happy. I was filled with reverence. We could be proud that a part of Laura was now sustaining someone else's life.

Trish herself was a gift to our family. Connecting with her created a positive way for us to mention Laura's name without provoking the pity we'd so often received. We could now share a sense of meaning in an otherwise meaningless tragedy. Each time we told the story, we heard a similar response; "I've got goose bumps."

Over the next weeks, Ron and Trish emailed back and forth and worked out a time when we could all meet. We thought a neutral spot would be best for introductions, and we chose Manhattan as our meeting place—Trish and Gary could drive from upstate New York in about the same amount of time as it would take us to fly from Milwaukee. As Ron made plans (and in line with my controlling tendencies), I helped him compose his emails: I wanted all the details to be just right, and, above all else, I didn't want to alienate Trish in any way. This was uncharted ground for all of us.

Seven months later, during the girls' spring break, we flew to New York City. Ron and I decided on staying in a hotel near Times Square, but we'd been careful to reserve a suite with a living room, rather than the typical one-room setup. We wanted Sara and Rachel to be able to retreat into the bedroom if the conversation became too emotional for them.

The four of us paced around the room, equal parts excited and nervous, as we waited for Trish and Gary to arrive. When we finally heard them knocking, Ron hurried across the room and opened the door. Trish smiled at us through her tears, and we all took turns greeting her and Gary with hugs. From the pictures Trish had sent us of herself, it felt like we already knew her well.

With the initial introductions over, we stood awkwardly in the middle of the hotel room and made polite small talk. When Ron asked Trish and Gary to sit down, I was taken aback as I saw a picture of Laura smiling at me through one of the clear plastic sleeves on Trish's tote bag: it took me a few seconds to remember that we'd sent her the photo. I was startled, but as soon as I'd caught my breath, I appreciated how deeply Laura was in Trish's thoughts.

We filled the first few minutes by recapping what we'd already learned from the Wisconsin Donor Network: the day after Laura was declared brain dead, her liver had been removed in the early morning hours. It was brought by ambulance—complete with flashing lights and sirens—to a waiting plane, then flown directly to New York.

Trish began telling us her own story. She'd been diagnosed with chronic myeloid leukemia in the spring of 2008. Doctors had treated her with medication, which worked well at first. "But about eight months after that, several teachers at my school told me my skin and eyes looked yellowish," she said. Trish's doctor immediately sent her to a local hospital, where she was told toxins were building up in her system—her body was essentially poisoning itself due to liver failure. "I changed into someone you wouldn't recognize," she admitted, astonished still at how powerfully her failing liver had affected her behavior. "I became so violent that the nurses had to restrain me." Her voice trembled as she spoke. "I soon fell into a coma. I don't remember anything else after that."

Trish paused and looked over at Gary. His face reddened before he cleared his throat and continued. "Trish was so sick that she was rushed by ambulance to Columbia-Presbyterian here in the city—the ride took three hours." Gary's voice quivered. "They told us there wasn't much they could do for her, except keep her comfortable." Because of her leukemia, Trish's medical team in Manhattan initially denied her a spot on the national transplant list—they were afraid her leukemia medications would interfere with the required post-transplant anti-rejection drugs. Trish's personal doctor believed otherwise: he drove to Manhattan and convinced the medical team that she was a viable transplant candidate.

"By that time," said Gary, "Trish was in such critical condition that she was placed first on the national transplant list." He paused and lowered his voice. "That Friday, the doctors began preparing her for a possible transplant even though a match hadn't been found. By Saturday evening, she was in really bad shape and was running out of time."

The alarm on Trish's phone buzzed. It was a reminder to take one of her thirty-three daily pills. She pulled a bottle of water and a daily pill organizer from her bag. Sara and Rachel watched wide-eyed as she took her pills. "It's all right," Trish told them. "They keep me healthy."

Gary continued. "On Sunday morning, I went to the hospital to say goodbye. When I arrived in the ICU, nurses were rushing around her bed in a frenzy. They were prepping Trish for surgery. A liver had become available!"

I looked over at Ron. He seemed hypnotized. The girls were, too. Trish was on the national transplant list for less than forty-eight hours before she'd received Laura's liver. On the same Sunday when we were planning Laura's funeral and *shiva*, Trish was undergoing her life-saving transplant.

"The surgery was supposed to take eight hours," Trish added, "but because the liver was such a good match, the operation only took four. When I woke up the next day, the surgeon told me it was meant to be."

"That was the day of Laura's funeral," Ron said.

Silence.

Stunned, I couldn't speak. I almost couldn't believe the timing.

On the day we'd buried our daughter, Trish had come back to life. Two intersecting lines on a graph with arrows pointing in opposite directions.

Soon, our conversation became more relaxed, and Trish asked us if we wanted to see her scar from the operation. She lifted her shirt, revealing a thick red line above her stomach. Sara and Rachel looked at the scar quickly and assured her it didn't seem "so bad." Trish smiled warmly. "I still have leukemia screenings every six months," she said, "but I'm in total remission, and there's no sign of any other cancer." I was relieved to hear that news.

Trish listened intently as Sara and Rachel proudly told her about their part in our family's decision to donate. She had an instant and natural rapport with the girls, almost as if she were a young aunt. Rachel, who was now eleven, had mostly avoided talking about the days when Laura was in the hospital, yet she now freely shared her own memories, some which Ron and I were hearing for the first time. Both our daughters had found a natural confidante in Trish, someone they immediately felt comfortable with.

When the conversation tapered off more than three hours later, I asked Gary to take a picture of our family with Trish, then we took a few others with just Trish, Sara, and Rachel. We were all a bit drained from the intensity of our conversation, but none of us were ready to say goodbye yet; we agreed to meet later for dinner. The girls then presented Trish with two beaded bracelets that they'd made for her before our trip. According to Sara, they gave her two bracelets in case she lost one, and to show her how much she meant to them.

For the next few hours, Ron, Sara, Rachel, and I walked around Manhattan's bustling streets. I was in a daze the whole time and could sense Laura's presence more strongly than usual. My brain flooded as I attempted to process my thoughts. I couldn't. It was too much to take in all at once.

Hours later, we all met at a nearby Italian restaurant; I purposely seated myself next to Trish after we'd been shown to our table. Ron ordered a beer and asked if anyone else would like a drink. Before Trish had a chance to answer, Sara teased her about not being old enough to drink since "Laura's liver is only fourteen years old." In an unexpectedly serious tone, Trish responded, "I don't drink. I appreciate my new liver too much for that."

Our conversation was surprisingly upbeat and casual. As I listened, I leaned back in my chair and realized that Ron's determination had made this day happen—he'd taken care of the paperwork and the details of our meeting. If he hadn't pushed me, we likely never would've met this wonderful person, this woman who we genuinely liked and who was almost literally related to us.

Before we ordered dessert, I turned to Trish and told her I didn't want her to feel obligated to us in any way. She paused, looking straight at me. "Don't worry," she began, "you have me for life." I lowered my eyes and smiled. The lump in my throat dissolved. I looked over at Sara and Rachel. Their smiles confirmed how much they liked Trish. Their smiles confirmed how much *Laura* would've liked Trish.

Significant gratitude washed over me as we walked back to our hotel. In most transplant cases, donor families and recipients never even meet, yet we were now developing a real relationship, a real friendship, with Trish. For as long as I could remember, I'd often wondered about my life's grand purpose—other than raising a family and being a good person—and I doubted if I'd ever find one. Now I knew I would never again need to question my reason for being: We had saved a life.

CHAPTER 14

Breathing Easier

May 2010 – February 2012

In May of 2010, after deferring the position for one year, I accepted the role of president of the MJF's Women's Division. By the time we'd received Trish's contact information in August, I'd thrown myself back into my work full-force and with a new focus: I actively recruited new board members, planned programs, and led strategic sessions. Many days I lost myself in my work, but spending time with MJF members was therapeutic, too. Before and after meetings, at coffee shops and over lunch, I'd seek out opportunities to talk about Laura and the insights our family had learned as we healed. In return, each woman—whether she was an old friend or a new acquaintance—would inevitably disclose her own life-challenges. As in the months after Laura's death, these authentic conversations were both my salve and my salvation, cathartic releases that propelled me through each day. My friends were my lifeline; talking with them allowed me to keep a positive focus overall. For me, the volunteering paradigm had been reversed. I'd given freely of my time for years, but I was now getting back more than I was giving—a shift that felt at once strange and welcome.

For me, serving as president was a way of recreating normalcy for our family. I also believed my volunteering had played an integral, and perhaps even inspirational, role throughout Sara and Rachel's lives. Retreating from the volunteering I felt so passionately about would've sent them the wrong message—that I was allowing our loss to define and diminish what mattered to me.

In my leadership role, I'd instinctively immersed myself in a welcoming and purpose-filled environment, yet I sensed others were surprised by the significant number of hours I spent at the MJF's offices. I was astonished, too, at the intensity of my commitment—I became more like a staff person than a lay volunteer. Looking back, I now better understand the fuel behind my passion: while making positive changes for the community, I also was channeling my restlessness and taking control of those aspects of life that were, in fact, controllable. By the time my yearlong term ended, I felt as if I'd made positive and hopefully lasting changes to the organization and its volunteers.

One week after the school year began, in September of 2011, Ron and I attended Nicolet's Back-to-School Night. The high school was a location full of triggers for us. Parents were invited to move through mini versions of their children's days, meet teachers, and learn about the curriculum for each class. When Ron and I picked up Sara's schedule from the information desk, we overheard a set of parents asking for two schedules—one for each of their two children—then watched as they split up to follow the two itineraries separately. A jolt hit me: two schedules weren't necessary for us. Ron grabbed my hand. We regrouped and made our way to Sara's first-period classroom.

In the hallways and classrooms, we passed many familiar faces. As usual, some parents avoided us while others greeted us with the pity-filled looks we'd become used to receiving. We'd both known the evening would be difficult, but we were committed to Sara's well-being—starting high school represented a big change for her and we wanted her to know we supported her, no matter what.

We went through Sara's condensed schedule eagerly. As I listened to each of her teachers, I thought about Sara's strengths, the subjects that would be her favorites, and the clubs she might join. For the most part, the night went smoothly until we reached her biology class. When Mr. S., who had also been Laura's teacher, explained the requirements for the upcoming annual science fair in February, a déjà vu-like sensation overpowered me. Less than two years earlier, Laura had put so much effort into her own project—the project she was never able to present. I bolted from my desk, past the rows of seated parents, and into the hallway.

As I leaned against a locker, a mom who knew me saw my tears and gave me a hug. Ron found me and asked if I wanted to go home. "No," I replied, "it wouldn't be fair to Sara if we left." It wouldn't have been fair to us, either: we had every right to participate fully in Sara's high school experience, to know her teachers, to guide her through her teen years, to be her proud parents.

That fall gave us a welcome opportunity to embrace both our surviving daughters' activities—and the hectic beauty of life. Sara's transition to high school was made easier because of the friends she made with the other players on the school's varsity tennis team. (Sara had been accepted onto the varsity team as an incoming freshman.) Throughout the season, I was happy to bring team snacks, help coordinate the end-of-the-season awards banquet, and most importantly, attend biweekly afterschool tennis matches and Saturday tournaments. On many weekends, Ron and I gladly sat in the bleachers, with Rachel often between us, while we watched Sara and her doubles partner face off against the opposing teams. Following the strict instructions for spectators, we did our best to restrain our cheers of excitement or sighs of dismay as we followed the ups and downs of each match. In the middle of October, when Sara and the entire Nicolet High School team advanced to the state tournament, our family traveled to Madison for two memorable weekends. Here, in this highly charged atmosphere, we were given the go-ahead to raucously root for Sara and her team.

Sara's matches immersed our family in an experience that felt different from what Laura's high school years would've looked like, which was liberating in a way that's hard to describe. During many games, our hearts were in our throats, although not from our all-too-familiar sadness, but from in-the-moment excitement.

As Sara took on a new confidence, Rachel began redefining herself as a preteen. One evening, I walked into the den and saw her playing a yoga game on her Nintendo Wii. As she followed the game's guided instructions, she contorted herself into exaggerated positions with a silliness much like Laura's. I told Rachel of the resemblance, but she shrugged off my comment as she continued to play—she already knew of the likeness. For me, as I watched Sara and Rachel mature, their mannerisms and resemblance to their older sister made me envision, in a bittersweet way, how Laura probably would've looked and acted as she grew. I was grateful that Sara and Rachel would always keep me connected to Laura in a physical way, even as they matured into young women in their own right.

As a middle-schooler, Rachel was sensitive to my fluctuating moods but mostly kept her thoughts and emotions to herself. She was our most laid-back and "in the moment" daughter, and she had her own way of processing her feelings—a way we needed to respect.

Rachel's fifth-grade year signaled a shift. When she was assigned to read *The Bridge to Terabithia*, the movie version of which she'd watched with Laura years earlier, her emotions finally broke through. Although Rachel knew that the novel's main character (a teenage girl) drowns, she threw the book across the living room when I walked in. "I'm not doing the assignment!" she yelled before running upstairs to my bedroom. She flung herself down on my bed and buried her head in a pillow. "It's not fair! I didn't have as much time with Laura as you, Dad, or Sara." The ferocity of Rachel's sobbing gutted me: I could never take away this awful truth. But I was also relieved that she seemed to be coming to terms with the grief and perhaps entering a new stage of healing.

Later that year, when Rachel asked, for the third time, to move into Laura's more-spacious bedroom—on the self-imposed condition that she would leave up Laura's pictures and posters—Ron and I hesitantly consented. We saw no reason to preserve the room as a shrine. Sara added her own conditions; chief among them was that the room always be referred to as "Laura's." Rachel quickly agreed. (When Rachel, Ron, or I accidentally forgot to refer to the room in this way, we would encounter Sara's fury.) To this day, Rachel still has a hard time articulating the many reasons why she wanted to move into Laura's room. Subconsciously, though, it must have been her way of staying connected to Laura, of finding a way to have "more time" with her sister.

Rachel found other ways of keeping connected to Laura. It wasn't long before she insisted on watching all eight seasons of *Desperate Housewives*, which had been Laura's favorite series from the time she'd entered eighth grade. Watching the show together as a family, despite its age-inappropriate content, was something we'd done every weekend. Initially, we kept up the Sunday-night tradition, but when two new characters—a mom named Laura Miller and her daughter, Rachel Miller—were introduced, the inexplicable coincidence had upset all of us, and Sara especially; from that night on, we stopped watching the program as a family. But since Rachel had been too young to really understand the show's more mature themes and plot points, she'd decided to watch the entire series in order to better understand the characters Laura had loved. I had reservations about Rachel binging on so much adult-oriented content, but I stopped myself from objecting; she was obviously determined to stay close to Laura in this way.

The first half of the school year flew by, and then the second semester kicked off with as much intensity as the first. Sara's freshman year had now progressed to almost the same point in the semester when Laura had begun complaining of headaches. I could sense Sara was on edge. She didn't know how Laura's classmates (who were now all juniors) would react to her in the hallways. When a senior girl actually mistook her for Laura one afternoon, Sara's anxiety only intensified.

Rachel also seemed understandably uneasy as the second semester began. Among other things, she'd been isolating herself in her bedroom and watching too many YouTube videos. Ron and I did all we could to make the transition easier for both of them. During these stressful January and February days, we often indulged with them in comfort foods and desserts, watched mindless TV shows and comedies, and—as needed—allowed both girls to take an occasional "mental health" day off from school.

On the morning of January 26, 2011—eleven days after Sara

turned fourteen-and-a-half years old—she came downstairs for breakfast and asked, "Mom, do you know I'm now older than Laura was?" Attempting to sound nonchalant even though I knew the significance of the date, I asked, "How does that make you feel?" I held my breath as I waited for her answer. "I don't know," Sara replied. "It's weird. I'm the oldest kid in our family now."

Although Sara was not our firstborn child, she was now unnaturally, but undeniably, our oldest daughter. Milestones, such as Sara surpassing the age that Laura never would, were events Ron and I both dreaded and then celebrated with a sigh of relief. These dates loomed large in our psyches, although we did make a conscious effort to focus on the positive. Even still, in the years to come, we breathed easier when Sara—and then Rachel—finished her freshman year, learned to drive, and graduated from high school. Since there were no more "guarantees," we had to learn to soak up happiness whenever and however we encountered it.

After Sara left for school that morning, I walked over to the table in our foyer and looked at the triptych of silver frames: every year, I inserted the girls' annual class photos into their dedicated slots. Sara and Rachel had new pictures from the fall, but Laura remained fourteen, forever smiling up at me. Time had stopped for her, but for me any change, regardless of how mundane, represented the severing of another connection to the world Laura had loved—whether it was her favorite frozen yogurt store closing or one of her middle school teachers retiring. In a way, these changes were exhausting, and I struggled to retrain myself to accept them more easily. Instead of viewing these breaks with the past as depressing, I needed to remember that life itself is change. No matter how hard I tried, I could never—and, on most levels, didn't want to—freeze time. Our lives couldn't stagnate. We couldn't let that happen.

Our deepening relationship with Trish gave me, and our entire family, a true reason to welcome change. More and more, Trish was becoming a part of our extended family and keeping us connected to Laura in surprising, positive ways. We "liked" Trish's posts on Facebook, wrote emails to her on her birthday, and sent her and Gary holiday cards. All four of us spoke with her by phone every few months—these calls were like mini family events that we all looked forward to. We felt indebted to her for her warmth and kindness, and she remained so appreciative of her new lease on life that we couldn't imagine a better "caretaker" for Laura's liver.

The rest of 2011, as well as early 2012, passed without too much drama. We still had our good days and our bad, but now the good days far outweighed the tough ones, and the "weirdness" of Laura's physical absence had generally subsided. In the frenzy of our everyday lives, I almost forgot, at times, that something so horrible had ever happened to us—a bizarre mind game, to put it mildly.

We still talked often about Laura—what she would've been doing had she lived, and how our lives might be different if she were still with us. We also tried our best to keep up our relationships with the parents of her classmates and friends. We followed their children's accomplishments on social media, and we also read their loving and poignant Facebook posts about Laura each year on her birthday and death anniversary. These messages uplifted us and filled us with pride.

The lead-up to the third anniversary of Laura's death was unsettling, but not quite as difficult as the first two. The day was made easier, too, by our newest tradition: after we'd met Trish in New York, we'd begun celebrating her "life anniversary" (one day after Laura had been declared brain dead). Having something so miraculously positive to focus on reminded us of all the good still in our lives. Time might not heal all wounds, but in our experience, the passing years did smooth out the rough edges.

CHAPTER 15

Stranger than Fiction

Fall 2012

M id-morning on *Yom Kippur*, at the end of September, I sat down on my bed and leaned over to put on my shoes. An intense, nauseating, painful wave surged through my forehead and into the back of my head. I collapsed back onto the mattress and waited for the sensation to fade. I reached for the Tylenol on my nightstand, then willed myself to go to services.

This wasn't the first headache that I'd had in recent weeks, although it certainly was the strongest and most alarming. Along with the headaches and dizzy spells, I'd also been unusually restless and irritable; little things—like Ron having accidentally booked the wrong hotel for one of our summer weekend getaways—made me unreasonably angry and I didn't know why. I'd attributed all these symptoms to stress: my father's MS was unfortunately progressing, Sara's junior-year tennis season had begun in August, and Rachel was in the midst of studying for her *bat mitzvah*, which would be in early November. I didn't have the time—or the desire—to worry about sporadic throbbing and lightheadedness. I mentioned my symptoms in passing to Ron, but not to Sara and Rachel. What would be the use of burdening the beginning of their school year with worry?

Rachel's *bat mitzvah* planning, in particular, had been weighing on me. Whether it was fair to Rachel or not, I associated Sara's *bat mitzvah*, three and a half years earlier, with trauma: I kept putting off making the arrangements for Rachel's celebration because I felt as if I were tempting fate. Rachel, who had always readily admitted to "not wanting to grow up too quickly," was also less enthused about becoming a *bat mitzvah* than either Laura or Sara had been. It was challenging to keep Rachel focused on preparing for an event I was secretly dreading, that I semi-consciously didn't believe would really happen. Too many decisions to make, too many projects to juggle. Even though I could reasonably blame my headaches and my increasingly high-strung state on these stresses, something still didn't feel right.

I also knew Rachel didn't need more pressure piled onto her understandable nervousness about publicly reading her *Torah* portion. I also didn't know if she associated Sara's *bat mitzvah* with the lead-up to her own. I imagined that she did, but I hesitated to broach the topic: if she wasn't already linking the two, I didn't want to unwittingly connect the dots for her.

A friend of mine—also named Sara—knew of my angst and offered to help. She emailed me theme ideas for the *bat mitzvah* party, went with me to the linen rental store, and helped me select place cards and centerpieces. I occasionally complained to her about my headaches, but I hid my concern about their increasing frequency. One afternoon at the local party supply store, I had trouble concentrating on what the salesperson was telling me. My brain was foggy, and none of the details seemed to matter. Sara urged me to sit down. I just wanted to go home and crawl into bed. A sense of panic crept through me: what was wrong with me?

I tolerated the headaches and brief dizziness in secret. When the pain surged in the middle of the night and early morning hours, I couldn't help but remember that Laura's headaches were also at their most intense at these times. A similarity too strong to ignore. A similarity that made all those sleepless nights after Laura's death seem all too real again.

At my annual checkup, my gynecologist attributed my symptoms to perimenopausal hormones and stress. She suggested nothing more than herbal supplements. I then scheduled an appointment with Laurie. (I'd been seeing her irregularly, but she understood why arranging Rachel's *bat mitzvah* was emotionally difficult.) Laurie listened intently, then reviewed some stress-management strategies. Neither of these appointments alleviated my concerns. I felt as if I were being dismissed, as if I'd suddenly become a hypochondriac.

I next went to see my primary care physician. She placed her hand on my arm and assured me that my symptoms were probably psychosomatic: just because Laura had been diagnosed with a brain tumor didn't mean I would too, and having two non-genetic brain tumors in one family was extremely improbable. When I mentioned other medical conditions that might be causing my headaches, my doctor didn't seem too concerned. She placated me by giving me a Xanax prescription to manage my anxiety, then handed me an order for an MRI scan. "You can get the test if you want," she said, "but I'm pretty sure there's nothing wrong with you."

In the weeks surrounding these doctor's appointments, Trish and Gary flew to Milwaukee for the first time to join us for our yearly memorial run/walk. Our family was in the second year of partnering with the Wolfe family, who had lost their young-adult son to a glioblastoma. The "Run with Wolfes" event attracted several hundred people, including approximately one hundred on the team we organized in memory of Laura.

Before Trish and Gary's visit, both girls had convinced Ron and me to hold a small welcome party at our home. (Sara had been particularly drawn to Trish's story and was especially interested in the ways Trish's recovery had inspired many to register to become potential organ donors). I was looking forward to seeing Trish and Gary, but even a small get-together added to my increasing stress—it was one more responsibility to manage while struggling with my headaches. Yet I pushed on, trying to remain positive. About an hour into the gathering, I walked back into the house after talking outside with some guests. I hadn't seen the girls—or Trish—for a little while and wondered where they were. I heard footsteps coming down the stairs. A moment later, all three of them entered the kitchen; Sara and Rachel had taken Trish on a tour of the house.

A shiver raced up my spine as the realization hit me: Trish had been inside Laura's room. That meant a piece of Laura—alive and well—had been in her old bedroom. My clashing emotions suddenly paralyzed me. I was upset that the girls hadn't asked me before bringing Trish upstairs, but at the same time an eerie astonishment washed over me—a sense of having come full circle, as if this instant in time had been predestined, as if Laura had come home. Ron, too, was stunned. Neither of us was completely shocked, though; in a way, we'd become accustomed to living the incomprehensible.

Once I collected myself, my thoughts kept returning to my own health for the rest of the afternoon. To what another crisis might mean to our family. To threatening our hard-won new normal. Part of me didn't want to know if anything was wrong with me; part of me could think of nothing else. Whereas in the past I'd relied so much on the company of others to soothe my nerves, now my reluctance to talk about my concerns made me feel isolated and scared.

As much as I now hate to admit it, I was relieved when Trish and Gary went back to New York. With the run/walk over, I could now focus my limited energy on getting through the fall and making it past Rachel's *bat mitzvah*. I needed to keep myself going: I was the mom—I was supposed to protect and prevent trauma, not be the source of it.

The next weeks were busy. Sara's tennis team had made it to the state finals for the third year in a row, and we again traveled to Madison for the tournament. Even knowing I was potentially risking my health, I couldn't bring myself to ruin the two most-anticipated weeks of Sara's season. I took more naps, drank more wine with dinner, and relied on several doses of Tylenol each day. I walked more slowly, avoided turning my head too quickly, and I was especially careful when getting in and out of the car. I powered through each day while putting off scheduling my MRI, afraid of learning what was wrong with me. I pretended that all was all right, even though my symptoms—and the sinking feeling in my gut—told me otherwise.

Soon, Rachel's *bat mitzvah* plans were in their final stages. As I sat in the parking lot waiting to pick up programs for the ceremony, I groaned from the pressure in my head. I was becoming convinced that we wouldn't make it through the *bat mitzvah* without something disastrous happening, either to myself or to a member of our family. Even so, I refused to focus on my well-being. There was too much to do. I was caught in a no-win situation: I couldn't risk having to cancel Rachel's ceremony because of a family health crisis. I refused to let that happen again, and certainly not on account of me.

I thought about my father's MS. Would he be healthy enough to attend Rachel's big day? I thought about Ron's parents, too, and (however illogically) wondered if they might be facing a health challenge that they hadn't told us about, something that would keep them from celebrating with Rachel. I tried to control my anxiety as fear whirred through my thoughts. If I'd learned anything from Sara's hastily rescheduled *bat mitzvah*, it was that being able to celebrate with loved ones was as important as the ritual itself—if not more so. Who would be absent this time? And what could I do to prevent it?

Rachel's *bat mitzvah* day arrived. Sitting on the *bimah* at the head of the sanctuary, I listened with pride and love as Rachel confidently chanted her prayers. I watched as our youngest, the baby of our family, entered into Jewish womanhood just as countless generations had done before her. When the service ended, Ron, Sara, Rachel, and I moved into the foyer to greet our guests for the *kiddush* lunch. I was relieved that we'd made it to the big day, but my pride for Rachel was mixed with dread. I hoped the doctors had been right: with all the related stress now behind me, maybe my symptoms would disappear.

That evening, as our guests were arriving for Rachel's party, I panned the community hall, admiring the brightly colored linens and balloon centerpieces. All looked as it should be. I asked the bartender for a glass of wine as Rachel and her friends began dancing under the strobe lights. Rachel looked so happy, as did our friends and family. Soon, the DJ pulled me onto the dance floor. I willed myself to dance for two songs, and I forced a smile for the photographer before escaping to a quiet hallway to rub my throbbing neck. I was relieved that I'd been able to push my health concerns aside so we could enjoy this milestone, just like every other Jewish family. Forging ahead, in spite of my fears, had been worth it.

The next afternoon, after a brunch at our home with our out-of-town guests, the house was quiet once again. Yet the peace only magnified my symptoms, which had not magically vanished as I'd hoped. My head throbbed. I used the feasible excuse of being tired from yesterday's events and went upstairs to lie down.

The next weekend, while I was out shopping, another wave of dizziness and pain hit me, this one so intense that I had to grab onto my cart to steady myself. I didn't want to cause a scene and closed my eyes until the surge passed. As soon as I felt stable enough, I slowly headed to the parking lot. I gingerly lowered myself into my car. I gripped the steering wheel with both hands and placed my head on it, unsure if I should be behind the wheel. I trembled as I drove home, reminding myself to breathe the whole way.

When I got home, I confessed to Ron—as my anxiety intensified—that I'd been minimizing, and essentially concealing, my headaches from him. "Susan, you need to get checked out," he said definitively. He was right. There was no more wishing the pain away, no more time to procrastinate. "You need to schedule the MRI and figure out what's going on," he insisted. He stared me down until I agreed to make an appointment right away.

I called my friend Barbara, whose husband Mark is a radiologist. She sensed my rising panic and figured out a way to squeeze me into Mark's schedule on Wednesday, three days away; she promised he would immediately share the findings with me. Ron agreed that we shouldn't mention the test to Sara or Rachel.

Mark pointed to the scans on his lightbox. "I'm sorry, Susan, but I can't sugarcoat it," he said, looking straight at me. "You have an aggressive brain tumor."

My heartbeat slowed as Mark's words became fuzzy. I grabbed the back of a chair to keep myself upright. Ron's face darkened. The word *aggressive* echoed in my head. Almost four years ago *aggressive* was the same word that was used to describe Laura's tumor, and she'd died within a few days. The walls began closing in on me. What we were hearing couldn't be real: it *couldn't* be. Yet I could see the evidence for myself in the large, glowing, amoeba-shaped area on my scan.

Mark waited until both Ron and I made eye contact with him before he continued. "I'm not certain, but it looks like a meningioma—a tumor that grows on the layer between the brain and skull." He paused, letting us recover again before giving us more information to take in. He explained that meningiomas are typically benign and usually asymptomatic—sometimes surgery isn't even necessary. "But since your tumor is very large and has been causing headaches," he concluded, "it needs to be removed."

"Removed," I thought. "I have an aggressive tumor that needs to be removed. Just like Laura." Mark's words reverberated in my head, yet I couldn't believe them. I *refused* to believe them. We'd worked so hard to stitch our lives back together . . . and now this? Life wasn't supposed to work this way. I'd almost forgotten how inexplicable and out of the blue Laura's death had been. How easily I'd forgotten that trauma occurs without warning.

Ron reached out and grabbed my hand. He and Mark began discussing the next steps, but I disengaged from the conversation—and the reality—until Mark called my primary care doctor. He reported the findings to her before handing me the phone.

"I'm so sorry, Susan. I never thought this could possibly happen," she said apologetically. "You need to go to the hospital. Right now."

CHAPTER 16

Thrust into Chaos (Again)

November 2012

T he drive to the hospital took only twenty minutes, but in that short time Ron and I—in our all-too-well-practiced crisis mode—called our parents, Barbara, Margie, Ruth, and a few other close friends. With each conversation, I couldn't believe the words streaming from my mouth. Terror seeped into my bones: how much time did I have left? Laura also had been diagnosed on a Wednesday morning; by that same evening she was on life support. Would that be my fate too? And didn't our family deserve a lifetime "get out of jail free card"? Hadn't we already paid our dues?

As soon as we reached the hospital's main entrance, Ron hugged me before assuring me that he would return as soon as he could. I didn't envy the task he had ahead of him: when Sara and Rachel came home from school, he'd have to blindside them with the news that their *mom* was now the one with the brain tumor.

I forced myself to walk through the hospital's glass doors, through the lobby, past the gift shop, and to the admissions desk. In a daze, I slid my insurance card under the glass window and confirmed my information. A man soon appeared with a wheelchair. He maneuvered me into an elevator, through a maze of fluorescent-lit hallways, and to the neurology unit. None of it seemed real.

In my room, I removed my earrings, my wedding ring, and Laura's Tiffany bracelet. I handed them to the nurse to lock up for safekeeping. As she left, I pulled back the plastic-like curtains of my room's window. With my eyes closed, I leaned my throbbing forehead on the cold glass; a moment later, I was shaken when I saw the children's hospital across the street—the place where Laura had died, a place I never wanted to see again, and especially not from my own hospital room.

The nurse returned and inserted an IV. I watched as the medicine dripped from the hanging bag, down through the clear tube, and into my arm. All at once, my reality was both incomprehensible and absurdly, yet cruelly, real. How could I be here? How could my family and I be thrust into chaos again?

Margie, unusually agitated and almost as shocked as I was, arrived and sat with me. Soon, the nurse handed me a clipboard with disclaimer forms. Without my reading glasses, I had difficulty seeing the small print. Unsure of what to do, I looked over at Margie. "Susan, just sign it," she said, an uncharacteristic quickness in her voice. "You need this surgery, *now*." She was right. I signed the forms immediately, without reading any further. I couldn't bring myself to begin considering the risks, couldn't allow myself to think of all that might go wrong, couldn't begin to accept the possibility of having a deadly brain tumor.

Laurie walked into my room a few minutes later. She'd driven to the hospital as soon as she'd heard my voicemail message. She was so alarmed that she very nearly drove the wrong way down an exit ramp in her rush to get to me. She insisted that I should've had her paged at her clinic. "If this doesn't qualify as an emergency," Laurie said, "I don't know what does."

Ron arrived with Sara a little while later. I was relieved to hear that Michelle, Margie's daughter, was staying at home with Rachel. At barely thirteen years old, Rachel was much too young for another trauma; Sara was, too, but at sixteen she was more emotionally mature and better able to understand the crisis we were facing. I still remember the shell-shocked look on Sara's face as she stood at the foot of my bed. Surreal fear filled the room.

The on-call neurosurgeon introduced himself to us within the hour. He calmly explained that the next day, a team of neuro-interventional radiologists would pinpoint the exact location of my tumor, then use an embolization technique to sever its blood supply. He'd scheduled me for a craniotomy on Friday, when he would remove as much of the mass as possible. He cautioned that two separate surgeries might be necessary because the tumor, which was on the left side of my brain, had grown so large that it was now pushing into my right hemisphere as well.

I must have turned white as he spoke, because he quickly assured me, "If you're going to have a brain tumor, a meningioma is the one to get. They're among the most common and treatable tumors." He was optimistic that the growth could be removed without impacting my optic, auditory, or frontal lobe functions. Because the tumor was near my motor cortex, his biggest concern was that I might experience some post-surgery deficits with my right leg. For all of his positivity, I didn't find much comfort in his words. I couldn't help but remember that Laura's initial prognosis had been positive as well.

I listened intently before I asked the question I was most afraid of hearing the answer to: "Did I make things worse by waiting so long?" He replied confidently, "No, the tumor has been growing for at least the past ten or fifteen years. Waiting a few extra weeks didn't cause any further damage." I breathed a sigh of relief even as my entire body shivered. I'd had a tumor for fifteen years: most of Laura's life, including the day she'd been diagnosed with hers.

The surgeon then explained that my tumor was in no way related to Laura's. I asked him about it several times, but he made it clear there was no medically known correlation between the two types, that nothing here was genetic or hereditary. Neither Ron nor I could believe his assurances, though—that answer didn't make any sense. How could this nightmare just be bad luck?

Later that night, Ron sent out an email with the news to more family and friends—many of whom we'd seen just ten days earlier at Rachel's *bat mitzvah*. "I thought your email had been hacked, or it was a bad joke," one friend responded. My college friend wrote, "My heart just sank when I read Ron's email. I didn't think this could be true. You guys have been through so much." Our teenage niece had a different kind of reaction, perhaps the most honest of them all: she'd thrown her phone across the room.

I appreciated the words of support, but still couldn't quite believe our family was once more the cause of concern. I couldn't fathom needing to call on our family and friends again, especially after they had already supported us so generously. Yet it was all brutally true. Every single part of it.

On Thursday, I underwent the embolization. The surgical team snaked a micro-camera, attached to a threaded catheter, up from my groin, through my carotid artery, and into my head. Even though I was under assault, I still cringe thinking about the procedure's invasiveness. The team successfully cauterized the tumor's blood flow, but I was unprepared for the agony afterward. Back in my room, pain seemed to reach every cell in my body, and I complained to a nurse that the aching in my head was at a twelve on a ten-point scale. As the night slowly passed, I watched the clock impatiently, waiting for the time when I could be given more pain medicine. I again thought about Laura. Was this how she felt when her headaches had become excruciating, when the emergency shunt was inserted? If she hadn't died so suddenly, how many more of these agonizing procedures would she have had to undergo?

Ron and my mom sat with me through the night. All they—and I—could do was pray that the doctors would do their best. All was out of our hands. We had to rely on our inner strength and faith to sustain us.

My mom later told me that I looked as gray that night as my dad had been after his open-heart operation (eleven years earlier). She didn't believe I'd be able to survive another surgery—especially a craniotomy—the next day. My mom struggled with the knowledge that rescheduling my surgery wasn't medically possible: with the cauterization complete, the tumor was dying and therefore needed to be removed within twenty-four hours.

In the morning, I was wheeled to the surgical suite. Ron, exhausted but steadfastly calm, followed me down the long corridors until we reached the entrance to the operating room. Time seemed to slow down as he bent over my gurney and kissed me. In those few unnaturally-long seconds, I considered the possibility of not surviving the operation. With a level-headedness that still dumbfounds me, I concluded that if I died, Ron would take good care of Sara and Rachel, and I would be with Laura. Suddenly, dying scared me less than before. If Laura could exist in whatever state or place came after death, why couldn't I?

Staring into the operating room's blinding lights, I surrendered all illusions of control. Life and death blurred together. I prayed that my family would stay strong if I died. As the anesthesiologist placed a mask over my mouth and nose, I inhaled deeply.

CHAPTER 17

Euphoric Insights

November – December 2012

Y ou're in post-op," the nurse said. "In a few minutes, we'll be taking you for a scan to see if the surgeon left any drill bits in your head." At the time, I didn't understand the joke, but I remember not caring. My headache was gone. I felt like myself, only better. "You can take me wherever you want. I've just survived brain surgery!" I thought ecstatically.

Ron appeared from behind the blue privacy curtain; unsure of my condition, he'd left the rest of the family in the waiting area. He'd expected me to be sedated and possibly unable to talk, not flying high on powerful steroids and giddy from just being alive. He was clearly shocked. "Come on in. Come in!" I shouted enthusiastically as I motioned for him to come closer. "I'm doing great!"

Ron went back to the waiting area to invite everyone to come to see me. My family had been given updates on my surgery at regular intervals; even so, the last five hours had been overwhelmingly stressful for them. My mom later told me she'd asked Ron several times, as they waited, how he was doing. Each time he gave her the same cautious, tempered response: "If Susan's okay, then I'm okay."

Specific memories from my first few post-surgery days are

etched in my mind: when Sara ran crying from my room after seeing the blood-stained bandage around my head; when my sister drove from Chicago to stay with me so Ron could get a full night's sleep; when I demanded that my brother (who had flown in from an overseas business trip) bring me a bagel and coffee from the cafeteria. Also seared in my memory is my father-in-law pacing at the foot of my bed, his head lowered to avoid eye contact. "Wipe that tear from your cheek," I remember teasing him. "It's so great," he'd said, referring to his elation at the operation's success. "It's so great."

Sara remembers more from that week than Rachel does. One of Sara's clearest memories is when a woman, who saw her crying alone in the hallway outside my recovery room, handed her a box of tissues. The anxious hours of waiting had, understandably, overpowered Sara. In spite of her being embarrassed at her breakdown, she remains grateful for this small gesture.

My neurosurgeon's concerns about complications on my right side proved correct. I was unable to wiggle the toes on my right foot or flex that ankle, and I had trouble taking more than two or three steps. I was surprised at my lack of concern: surviving brain surgery trumped everything else.

On the third day, a nurse handed me a mirror before she removed the gauze bandage from my head. I saw my eyes widen in the mirror: I looked like an alien from a low-budget movie. Bloodstained metal staples began at my hairline and continued in a row to the back of my head. The left side of my skull was sunken and flat. A bald patch surrounded the incision, and what remained of my unwashed hair fell limply at my shoulders. I pleaded with the nurse to shave off the rest of my hair.

The on-staff physical therapist helped me out of bed later that afternoon. She stabilized my calf and foot with a plastic brace, placed a cloth strap around my waist to safeguard me from falling, and then handed me a walker. As she assessed my motor skills, I asked her to tell me stories of other women around my age who had undergone similar surgeries, but my story was anything but common. With great effort, I unsteadily walked down the hallway and back before collapsing into bed, thankful to be forty-seven years old, not eighty-seven.

Six days after being admitted, I was released from the hospital. Mercifully, there was no need for a second surgery, and the initial pathology indicated that the tumor had been benign. Ron drove slower than usual on the ride home, yet with each bump and curve I moaned: my brain felt like a chandelier swaying in a windstorm. I gazed out at the Milwaukee skyline and felt both exhilarated and exhausted, as if I were returning to school after having the flu for a week.

At home, Ron carefully guided me to the couch in the den. He covered me with a blanket, Sara cradled my head in her lap, and Rachel cuddled beside me. Life was even better than before. No more tennis matches to attend, *bat mitzvahs* to plan, or parties to host. But most importantly, no more headaches. I sighed contentedly and gave myself permission to recover. To simply be: that was enough.

Ron took me to my first physical therapy appointment the next morning. Pumped full of steroids, I felt like Superwoman yet required Ron's help getting out of the car. With him at my side, I gripped my walker and shuffled through the lobby's long hallway. The receptionist couldn't locate my records because they hadn't yet been transferred from the hospital. "We usually don't see patients this soon," she said, glancing at my arms; they still showed adhesive-tape residue and telltale bruises from my IVs. "Wow. You're fresh."

I've since asked Ron why he made my first physical therapy appointment so soon after my release. He reminded me that it had been my idea, not his: from my hospital bed, I'd insisted he schedule the appointment as soon as possible. Apparently, I was determined, right from the start, to regain my health and reclaim my life.

The next day was Thanksgiving. In a medication-induced state, I was content to sit by myself and practice wiggling my toes and flexing my feet. I prayed for others who'd been through the same surgery but who might not have fared as well as I had. I watched the Macy's Day Parade and imagined myself as one of the balloon characters floating above humankind.

Nearly every year, Ron and I had hosted a traditional Thanksgiving dinner for both of our extended families. This year, however, only my parents drove up from Evanston. Ron reheated a restaurant-prepared meal, which a friend had generously ordered for us. Ron, Sara, Rachel, and my dad ate in the dining room, while my mom and I ate in the quiet of the den. I held my mom's hand and rested my head on her shoulder. The evening resembled little of a Norman Rockwell family dinner, but it made no difference; I doubt I'll ever have a more meaningful Thanksgiving.

Everyday tasks now became exceptionally taxing, including doing all the simple things I'd always taken for granted. Morning sponge baths (to avoid wetting the staples in my scalp) became the norm, and the few times I did shower, Ron had to guide me as I stepped over the shower's three-inch lip, then carefully lower me onto a metal folding chair he'd placed in the stall. Getting dressed became an event. Making it downstairs felt like an accomplishment. With each step I took, as I leaned on my walker,

I concentrated on making sure my right foot didn't drag behind me. The few times I ventured outside, either Sara or Rachel held me tightly as I shuffled across the icy pavement.

I'd been given little information about how I would feel after the surgery, and even if I had, I don't think I could've predicted the manic highs caused by the steroids. I felt proud of being a member of the "brain tumor survivor" club. In my excitement, I searched online for an "I survived brain surgery" T-shirt; I found more options than I was expecting, and Ron placed the order for me. (A few weeks later, I learned from an acquaintance that her husband, who had also had a meningioma removed, collects humorous brain-surgery-related items, including baseball caps and gelatin molds.) But most of all, I was elated, enjoying the euphoria, grateful to be alive, and wonderfully free from headaches.

Exactly one week after my release from the hospital, Ron wheeled me down the hallway toward my surgeon's office for my first follow-up appointment. We were learning the tumor's final pathology today. While we'd been told that the tumor was most likely benign, the words "most likely" hadn't reassured us: we knew all too well that statistics don't mean much if you're the atypical, unlucky patient. If my tumor had been malignant, I would need radiation treatments, which would come with the risk of serious side effects. The uncertainty was the only worry that had managed to penetrate my idyllic "permission to recover" state. I'd been so nervous that morning that I'd taken a Xanax to calm my nerves; Ron did not have that benefit.

In the waiting room, an older woman was seated across from me. I wondered about her reason for being here. She looked healthy enough, but perhaps her appointment was a pre-surgical consult to map out her own operation. Because my craniotomy had been an emergency surgery, I'd been likely spared months of pre-op appointments and the associated fears. I was beyond grateful that my operation was behind me. I said a quick prayer for her future good health and one for myself as well.

Time seemed to stand still as we waited. I unfolded and refolded the typewritten, double-sided page of questions we'd compiled the night before. At my appointment time, a nurse came out and called another patient's name. I looked at Ron. "It's our turn. I can't wait any longer," I hissed. "Susan, there's nothing we can do," he responded impatiently. He was right, of course, but that didn't ease my nerves—or his.

Twenty minutes later, a nurse guided us into an exam room. We waited some more. Ron turned on the voice-memo app on his phone so we could record the appointment. I stared at the brain diagrams on the walls: a chill ran through me as I thought about the surgeons cutting into my skull, about the tumor that I'd been harboring for more than a decade, about the cancer risk, about potential long-term brain damage.

The door finally opened. "The pathology is beautiful," my surgeon announced happily. Ron squeezed my hand and his shoulders relaxed. I released a breath I hadn't even been aware I was holding. No cancer. Whatever else came next, my family and I wouldn't have to face a deadly brain cancer again.

We started to discuss our list of questions. My surgeon assured us that the tumor would probably never grow back; if it did return, my yearly follow-up MRIs would catch it early. He told us that it wasn't uncommon for people to live for years with meningiomas and not know it[4]—sometimes a tumor would only be discovered during an autopsy after a patient had died from unrelated causes.

_____

4. See <http://neurosurgery.ucla.edu/meningioma-brain-tumor> for more information.

Yet because my tumor had been, in my surgeon's words, "the size of a crushed orange," it needed to be removed as soon as it was discovered.

The news was encouraging, but I had other questions as well. "Will my head ever even out?" I asked, pointing to the still-flattened area on my left side. He told me that my cerebral fluid would mostly fill in the void over time, but that my head would never completely regain its shape—the tumor had eroded the bone on my left side too much for him to reattach that part of my skull. At this last statement, my face must've reflected my shock, because he quickly added, "We used titanium mesh to protect your brain. Titanium is very durable. It's used to make airplane wings."

Relative to the circumstances, I was given a clean bill of health. I was told not to drive for three months, and I was encouraged to continue physical therapy to regain my strength and retrain my right foot. Just when I was about to breathe a sigh of relief, my surgeon said something that made me question the last few years of my life: "Because you had the tumor for so long," he began, "it's possible that it affected your focus, memory, and emotions without your realizing it."

I was stunned. Had this tumor taken a toll on my patience and attention span—or, even more likely, intensified my years of grieving? How greatly had it affected my ability to cope with losing Laura? Was that why I'd felt so overwhelmed, so alone, in my pain?

Ron asked a few follow-up questions while I leaned back in my chair and processed my thoughts. I decided to keep them to myself: after all, I'd just been given the best possible prognosis. I would be okay. My family would be okay. I still had a long recovery road ahead of me, but I could be thankful for that much.

At the end of the appointment, I stood up, with effort, and hugged my surgeon. "You've given me a miracle," I told him. Ron took a picture of us together, which I would use as my phone's background for the next few months. My surgeon was my hero. "I always celebrate good news," he told us. "Have yourselves a nice dinner tonight."

As we left his office, the world seemed lighter. I looked out of the large windows lining the hallway as Ron wheeled me toward the elevator; huge snowflakes swirled through the air, descending as if in slow motion and blanketing the grass below. Life was good.

When Rachel came home from school each day, she would cuddle up to me on the couch. I soaked up the warmth of her body and felt how deeply I was loved. Instead of my mothering her, Rachel "daughtered" me: she was so attuned to my moods and needs that whenever I became cranky, she suggested I take a nap. Ron took good care of me as well. He helped me tie scarves over my shaved head, made me a dessert plate each night to satisfy my sweet tooth, and listened to my many middle-of-the-night reflections on life despite his needing to go to work in the morning. His closeness felt like a security blanket of hope.

Because my recovery would take months, we used the calendar-based website Lotsa Helping Hands to enable friends and family to volunteer—on their own schedule—to help with everyday essentials like staying with me during the day, driving me to physical therapy, or shuttling Rachel to her afterschool programs (something which Rachel quickly tired of). As friends streamed into the den daily, I realized once again how blessed I was to have so many strong relationships.

My appetite surged, and—because of both the steroids and my

own need for comfort—I indulged in extraordinary amounts of food. I told myself that this was no time for dieting, that my brain needed fuel to heal. I ate seconds of meals I'd never particularly liked (such as pot roast and potatoes), and I wolfed down the smoothies and deli sandwiches my friends brought me. Even now, we still laugh about the afternoon when, after finishing my own slice of tiramisu, I eyed Margie's uneaten piece. (Without a word, she'd slid her plate toward me as she and Ron traded smiles.) Ultimately, though, my appetite proved to be a mixed blessing; it enabled my recovery but also caused me to gain fifteen pounds.

Freed from the burden of obligations, expectations, and everyday restraints and demands, I felt unencumbered, like a freewheeling kite floating through a boundless ether. I didn't know whether my euphoria was from the steroids, or from the learning I'd done through grieving for Laura for almost four years. I didn't care, either way. I remained overjoyed and energized by the freedom to recover. No longer was my mind trapped in a perpetual loop of activity and anxiety, no longer did I need a "grand purpose" in life to feel validated. Instead of striving to achieve, I could just be. I had nothing to prove to anybody. I let go of self-judgment. Living itself, surrounded by family and friends, became purpose enough.

In those first few mostly-housebound weeks, I perceived myself as the center of attention. As friends again came selflessly to our aid, my bonds with them became more important than ever to me—so much so that I sensed our fundamental human interconnectedness. Losing Laura had taught me how reaching out in times of adversity is crucial to sustaining and strengthening each other, but now, with so many people supporting me for the second time, I understood it on an even deeper level. In these precious and healing weeks with my friends, I recounted the details from my most recent—and again inexplicable—trauma, and I spoke about my life-realizations about gratitude, friendship, and compassion.

Once again, talking helped me heal. Covered with fleece blankets and nestled on the couch, I proclaimed "The Truth According to Susan" and zealously revealed my insights into life's "big questions." I felt as though I'd pulled back the curtain which separates us from each other in our daily lives. I'm sure I sounded like a New Age guru, yet I sensed, in each cell of my body, the truth behind my words. I had entered a dimension where the trivial was swept away and replaced by gratitude, kindness, compassion, and love—a circle of authentic caring, where I could be vulnerable yet safe. A state I never wanted to end.

I declared that I wanted to write a book called *Brain Surgery: The Best Thing That Ever Happened to Me.* I was vaguely aware of how bizarre I sounded, yet I didn't care. Just like when Laura had passed, I imagined that my friends were learning through me without having to actually suffer themselves. From my vantage point, they all seemed to gaze at me with an intensity that indicated a desire to find deeper meaning in their own lives. In retrospect, I'm convinced my friends left my house thinking, "I want whatever drugs she's taking!"

Medicated or not, every word of my revelations still feels true today; while the nirvana-like feeling of the steroids certainly amplified my perceptions, the insights were my own and were most likely birthed from my past struggles. By confronting my painful emotions and candidly sharing my stories in the aftermath of Laura's death, I'd progressed up a steep learning curve; surviving the trauma of my craniotomy had pushed me into a new and deep-rooted type of awareness.

CHAPTER 18

Learning to Skip

Winter 2012 - Spring 2013

As my friend Barbara pulled into my driveway after driving me home from physical therapy, something dangling from Laura's memorial crab apple tree caught my eye. It looked as if the branches were covered in holiday ornaments. After limping across the snow-covered yard, I reached up and grabbed a knitted maroon hat from the lowest branch. Barbara removed the rest of the homemade hats from the other branches. Overwhelmed by the unexpected display, I was speechless.

I realized, within a few minutes, that my neighbor Heidi (who'd recently offered to teach me to knit) had probably arranged the surprise. When I called her, she admitted to being the culprit. She'd organized a group of women—some who knew me and others who didn't—to knit a creative assortment of caps; she'd wanted them to look as if they had sprouted from Laura's tree. As I tried on each of the caringly-crafted hats, I thought about the love and effort behind each handmade creation.

When I showed the hats to Sara and Rachel, they were both impressed by my new collection and relieved that I would now be more likely to conceal my shaved head and still-healing wound. They'd been much more disturbed by my fresh scar and misshapen head than I'd been—I cared so little about my appearance that I'd never even considered buying a wig.

Within those initial recovery weeks, I graduated sooner than expected from a walker to a cane, but, even so, simple activities (such as walking to the end of our driveway and back) often left me drained, hungry, and in need of another dose of pain medicine. I still had difficulty with my leg-strengthening exercises. While moving through the alphabet and creating "air letters" with my ankle and foot, my energy would fade after the letter *K*. At my physical therapy appointments, basic arm exercises, like lifting a one-pound wooden stick over my head ten times, seemed as if they were Olympic feats, and one afternoon I burst into tears during a simple, timed pegboard exercise.

I remained fragile. I remember many car rides when I would place a pillow around my head to cushion my still-sensitive brain from the normal bumps in the road; I also needed to shield my eyes from oncoming headlights. On these rides especially, I thought about my life, which had once again been overturned by trauma and put on hold while others moved forward as normal. I was becoming tired of this pattern, yet I was still strangely proud and filled with a new self-confidence. With each day, I grew more determined to do whatever was needed to regain my strength and reclaim my life.

As I was weaned off the steroids, my "Truth According to Susan" revelations diminished. What continued, though, was my self-obsessiveness: my own needs and desires—I'm ashamed to admit—took precedence over everyone else's. I didn't know at the time just how insensitive I was being. Even basic courtesies were beyond me; I'm embarrassed to confess that when Ron's parents visited one day, I ignored them almost completely. Playing sudoku by myself seemed much more appealing.

As with many patients recovering from craniotomies, my senses were heightened. One weekend afternoon, when Rachel snuggled up beside me on the sofa, I blurted out, "You smell. You need to take a shower." Understandably shocked, she ran crying from the room, and Ron was upset as well. However, neither reaction had a lasting effect on me, because I made the same offensive comment to Sara fifteen minutes later when she, too, sat down next to me. A few days later, I pushed Ron beyond his limit of almost-infinite patience when I demanded—as if he were my butler—that he make me a turkey sandwich "with the bread from Kaufman's Deli. No mayo, but with mustard, lettuce, and chocolate *rugelach* for dessert." He'd justifiably snapped at me in reply.

Looking back, I can see that my behavior was much like my dad's. In addition to MS, he was also suffering from Lewy body dementia and would often become infuriated when he didn't immediately get what he wanted. I now better understand his inability to regulate his emotions, because I experienced nearly the same lack of control.

As hard as it is to admit, I paid uncharacteristically little attention to Sara and Rachel during this time. As they recounted their days, their lives seemed too far removed from my cocoon on the sofa to capture my interest. Without even realizing it, I was now hoarding for myself the energy I'd once poured so intensely into Laura, Sara, and Rachel.

I was so self-absorbed that I scarcely noticed Sara's intensifying interest in promoting organ donation programs. She'd recently received her driver's license, and her frustration with the outdated information she'd received during the state-mandated organ-donation session made her more determined than ever to raise awareness about the shortage of organs. Under any normal circumstances, I would've been very proud of her and far more encouraging, yet I felt detached as Sara brainstormed ways to encourage other Wisconsin high school students to sign the back of their licenses and become potential donors.

Ron confronted me one day when we were alone in the house. He pleaded with me to refocus and give more attention to Sara and Rachel. "I understand you're still recovering," he said, "but you're ignoring the girls. You have to start acting like their mom again." The truth of his words stung, but they snapped me out of my post-surgical self-centeredness, and I began giving my daughters the attention and support they deserved.

Sara and Rachel still tease me about my demanding outbursts. What I'd perceived as a few weeks of a mostly blissful recovery period, my family recalls as a few *months* of dealing with my self-centeredness. Years later, Ron told me how disorienting my behavior had been. "You didn't care what was happening in our lives," he said. "We understood, but it wasn't easy."

During my recovery, Ron went above and beyond upholding the "in sickness and in health" marriage vow. He saw me at my worst, at my most dependent and vulnerable, yet he never wavered once. Even now, his calm, steadfast support still awes me. When Laura died, Ron allowed me to grieve without judgment, and then—only a few years later—he was again responsible for caring for the girls (and for me) when I could not. If the situations are ever reversed, I hope I'll be able to do as well by him.

After two months of outpatient physical and occupational therapy, I graduated to working with Abby, a personal trainer at the JCC. My routine included lifting light weights, doing modified sit-ups, and walking slowly on the treadmill. Abby listened to my fears and worries, and she cheered me on during our sessions. I remember being cautious and unsure of my physical limitations, and although Abby assured me that exertion wouldn't cause a blood vessel in my head to explode, I knew neither of us could say that with complete confidence. Not in this "no guarantees" world.

I watched as Abby's older clients performed their exercises with seeming ease, while I still had to hold onto my treadmill's side rails in case my drop foot caused me to lose my balance. Some days I struggled with the idea that I'd become old before my time, that my body had somehow cheated me out of years of good health. Abby assisted me as I relearned how to lunge, hop, and slowly jog in place, but even after many months of work, I was still unable to skip. My right foot lacked the power to lift me upward and propel me forward at the same time; it would be a long time before I finally did learn to skip again.

While at lunch with Ruth one day, I complained in frustration about not yet being able to do this one simple kindergarten-like activity. "Why do you care about skipping?" she asked. I didn't have a good, easily explainable, answer, and I wondered what had happened to my initial overwhelming gratitude for simply being alive.

Similarly, I'd become fixated on a minor concern—a surgical abrasion above my left eyebrow. One evening, as I was examining the scar in the bathroom mirror, Rachel asked, "Mom, you had brain surgery—why do you care about something so small?" Once again, I couldn't quite verbalize my feelings, but now I grasped the reason: it was infinitely easier to understand insignificant physical deficits and imperfections than my invasive and risky emergency surgery.

After almost three months of not driving, I was thrilled at

the thought of taking myself—without help—to physical therapy appointments, volunteer meetings, or the grocery store. I could now begin relying less on the generosity of my friends and neighbors, and I could begin feeling more like myself. When I finally got behind the wheel, driving itself seemed like an extraordinary freedom. I was, once again, reclaiming my life and independence.

On one of the first days after I began driving again, I took Sara to her dental appointment, met a friend for lunch, and then headed out to pick Rachel up from school later in the afternoon. As I turned onto a side street a few blocks from home, the muscles in my right leg suddenly—without any warning—contracted and released violently. I hit the brake as I pulled the car over. Just as I came to a stop, an electric current exploded through my foot, snaked up my leg, and shot through my neck and head. My right elbow jerked, and my hand curled in uncontrollably toward my chest. Ultimately, the entire right side of my body began spasming. One thought flooded my mind: My life will never be the same.

With my left arm, I honked the horn wildly. With my still-shaking right hand, I dialed 911 on my phone. I looked into the rearview mirror and forced a smile, testing to see if it was crooked—a sign that I was having a stroke. I prayed I would stay conscious until help arrived. I panicked as I thought about what could possibly be wrong with me: had my three months of progress now been obliterated?

The spasms dwindled to small tremors, after ten agonizingly long minutes. An ambulance and two police cars arrived. A paramedic administered oxygen and then began peppering me with questions. "I need to pick up my daughter from middle school,"

I blurted out. One of the policemen offered to send a cruiser to pick Rachel up. "No! She'll be too scared if she sees a police car!" Just then, a second policeman asked, "Ma'am, do you have an anxiety issue?"

Even in the chaos, I almost laughed. I thought to myself, "My daughter died from a brain tumor, and I had brain surgery three months ago. Why *wouldn't* I have anxiety?" I kept my thought to myself, though, and wished that I'd brought my Xanax with me.

A neighbor, who was out walking his dog, offered to get Rachel from school and bring her to his house. I thanked him before quickly calling both Ron and Margie. The paramedics then lifted me into the ambulance, and I spent the ride to the hospital pressing down on my restless right leg and terrified of the thought of my body short-circuiting again.

With a parched throat and a still-erratically-jerking leg, I was propelled through the emergency room's doors. Jumbled memories from my hospital stay—and Laura's—flooded my mind. After a brief exam and scan, a doctor told me that I'd had a seizure, which most likely had been caused by the scarring around my motor cortex. She then handed me a prescription for the same anti-seizure medicine I'd been weaned from six weeks earlier. I'd experienced a primary focal seizure—if I'd had a more serious generalized tonic-clonic seizure, I would've lost full control of my body and could have blacked out behind the wheel. The thought was too frightening to think about.

Since I was prohibited from driving for yet another three months, I had no choice but to swallow my pride and disappointment and once again accept daily help—something that I thought was behind me. I hoped I would eventually regain the ability to drive. I hoped I would regain the *confidence* to drive without the fear of killing myself or someone else.

Although I never suffered another full-blown seizure, my right leg would, on occasion, contract and feel as if it were suddenly wooden. Whether we were at a family celebration or out to dinner with friends, I never knew when my body would betray me—and I never knew if these spasms were the start of another seizure. With time, I learned the triggers: cold and windy winter nights, vigorous exercise, thunderstorms, or even becoming impassioned about a topic. Some of these situations I could control, but many I couldn't avoid or even predict. My newly-compromised nervous system trapped me in a cruel mind game—from minute to minute, I worried about my brain's synapses failing me again. The ultimate vulnerability.

Susan in recovery—December 2012

Trish, Sara, and Rachel—O'Neill family cottage (Pennsylvania)
—May 2015

Laura Miller Memorial Team at eighth annual
"Run with Wolfes" event—Fall 2017

Ron, Rachel, Sara, and Susan at "Run with Wolfes" event—Fall 2017

CHAPTER 19

Choosing My Response

Summer 2013

No matter how much I tried, my newly-heightened and pervasive anxiety couldn't be managed with medication. I needed something more than drugs to reclaim my equilibrium. My neuropsychologist friend was empathetic and offered her professional opinion; in her view, being blindsided by my tumor when I'd already been traumatized by Laura's diagnosis and death was akin to an extreme form of exposure therapy.

Exposure therapy, I learned, is a behavioral technique that exposes trauma survivors to circumstances similar to those of their own traumatic experiences; from this, survivors become desensitized to associated fears.[5] My friend's explanation resonated with me. I went over the similarities between Laura's medical crisis and my own: both tumors were completely unforeseen; we were both hospitalized on a Wednesday with our surgeries being scheduled for a Friday; we both had been surrounded by concerned friends and family; and, in my case, I was cared for by many of the same people who'd come to our family's aid after Laura's death. The parallels swirled together in perplexing ways—I almost didn't believe them myself.

---

5. See <http://www.psychiatrictimes.com/anxiety/exposure-therapy-anxety -disorders> for more information.

I knew I needed help processing my increasingly scattered and muddled thoughts, so I called my friend Susan who taught mindfulness and meditation in the Milwaukee public schools. She told me that trauma triggers the brain's stress response. Repeated trauma and other ongoing hyper-stressors can have physical, long-lasting effects on the brain, particularly on the amygdala, which regulates the brain's fight-or-flight response.[6] She suggested that meditation could bring me calm, untangle my thoughts, help me live more fully in the present, and possibly rebalance any hypersensitivity in my amygdala.[7] She then coached me on the basics of directed, diaphragmatic breathing. As amazing as it seems, directed breathing re-engages our frontal cortex and influences our entire nervous system, which can lower our heart rate, relax our mind, reduce cortisol levels, and over time, help us to return to a healthier equilibrium.[8]

Susan also explained that being mindful, or self-aware of our emotions, can teach us to be more forgiving of ourselves, to adapt to new situations with intention, and to develop our resilience. We can teach our brains to be more resilient, she added, but only if we engage with the struggle and purposefully seek change. She cited books by Dr. Jon Kabat-Zinn, lent me her guided body-scan meditations, and invited me to attend her upcoming *Growing Minds* meditation class, which she co-taught with her colleague Anna.

After we talked, I realized that for most of my life I'd been

---

6. See <www.health.harvard.edu/staying-healthy/understanding-the-stress-response> for more information.

7. See <https://www.mindful.org/how-the-brain-changes-when-you-meditate> for more information.

8. See <www.ncbi.nlm.nih.gov/pmc/articles/PMC5455070> for more information.

either anticipating the future or reflecting on the past—I'd rarely felt grounded in the here and now. Being present in the moment had always seemed unattainable to me, yet because I was now more determined than ever to regain a healthy emotional balance, I believed mindfulness and meditation might help.

"Don't struggle against the discomfort," Anna encouraged in a firm, gentle voice. "Explore the pain with curiosity."

Like the other students in our mindfulness class, and with my eyes closed, I focused my attention on the hot pepper slice I was holding against my lips. I concentrated on accepting the pain and moving through it. Not fighting against the burning sensation made the pepper's heat manageable, easier to tolerate.

In this first session, our class of twenty women was encouraged to perceive our emotions and thoughts as clouds passing by, clouds that soon would be replaced by other feelings and observations, and then others. Embracing the fleeting nature of my emotions reminded me of the Hebrew phrase, "*Gam zeh ya'avor*." ("This too shall pass.") I focused on appreciating the here and now and on remembering to breathe. I inhaled deeply for six seconds, then exhaled slowly for a count of ten.

After reading about meditation and mindfulness at home, I'd signed up for this six-week *Growing Minds* session at a nearby synagogue. The floor-to-ceiling windows in the community room created a safe space for us to take in each of the session's varied topics: gratitude, appreciating each moment, releasing self-doubt. We were introduced to concepts such as making peace with impermanence, increasing self-awareness and regulating our emotions, and not trying to control the uncontrollable. We were encouraged to give ourselves permission to "be" where we were in life, free of judgments, expectations, or guilt. We were told to be at ease with ourselves, become centered, and to eliminate our critical inner voice.

At the end of each session, we were given "homework" to help us practice each lesson in our everyday lives. Some exercises, like turning off the air conditioning and instead rolling down the car window to appreciate the breeze, were simple yet eye-opening. Others, such as taking a moment to acknowledge and control my irritation before pointlessly snapping at Ron, were more challenging. I knew I would have to practice if I truly wanted to achieve a higher sense of serenity.

In my conversations with Susan outside of class, we talked about many topics, such as life's chaotic and unknowable nature. She explained that, in contrast to my upbringing, I'd have to fully accept the idea that few things were truly within my control—a concept she could see I was still struggling with. Susan recommended that I strive toward balance; that balance, she counseled, would come from managing my *immediate* responses to triggers and other stressors.

"May I be happy, may I be healthy, may I be free of worry, may I have peace." As I lay stretched out on a yoga mat during another session, these powerful mantras of self-compassion washed over me. I thought about the eerie parallels between my tumor and Laura's, but now—instead of looking for similarities—I recounted the differences. Our diagnoses, which both shared the words *brain tumor*, were, in fact, dissimilar and unrelated: my benign tumor had originated on my meninges (the brain's outer protective membrane), whereas Laura's tumor—rare, cancerous, and incurable—had grown deep within her cerebellum. In spite of my believing the two conditions were cosmically linked and intertwined the two of us even more closely, the medical risks, expected outcomes, and mortality rates differed significantly. As Laura's mom, I'd felt guilty for having lived when she had not; now, as a brain tumor survivor, that guilt had resurfaced in ways that my new meditation techniques were helping me recognize and address.

As I exhaled, I finally internalized two basic truths: four years earlier, there was nothing Ron or I could have done to save Laura; the previous year, there also was nothing I could've done to prevent my terrifying, yet much less severe, diagnosis. I'd told myself both these things countless times, but this was different. This time they reached the deepest recesses of my mind and being.

I breathed in again for a count of six. As I slowly exhaled, a serenity swept through my body. I suddenly felt an overpowering release: I was done being miserable. Done with feeling guilty about Laura's dying and our surviving. Done with being scared of my own death, done with being scared of death for her. I'd been given a second chance at life, and by sharing my own story I was now creating a purpose for myself other than grieving: I was done feeling guilty about that as well.

An epiphany opened my mind and soul: instead of grasping backward and struggling to haul memories of Laura forward, I could now walk arm in arm with her, essentially holding her hand in mine, with her spirit embedded within me. I'd been blessed to have Laura as my daughter—she'd loved Ron and me to the moon, and we loved her to the moon and back. My memories and my ongoing love for Laura would have to be enough. I could choose to focus on the beautiful, intensely positive impact she would always have on our family—and on Trish's. I wouldn't miss Laura any less, but I could now feel more at peace knowing that she'd always be with me. I could now be more at peace with my own survival, more at peace with embracing my life and its meaning. Something within me shifted in that moment: I finally gave myself permission to thrive.

That evening, I went home uplifted. "Laura's death is lighter for me now," I told Ron. "Well, it's not for me," he answered, with hurt and anger in his voice. He looked away from me—I had tread on sacred ground. He didn't understand my new perspective. How could he? My experience wasn't his, and his not mine.

Ron and I had twice faced the unimaginable together, yet for all his loving support, I was the one who'd had the tumor, I was the one whose survival was threatened, and I was the one who'd fought to bring myself back to a healthy state. How could I ever have expected Ron—or anyone else—to feel my immediate post-surgery ecstasy and self-confidence, or to experience my epiphany alongside me? The answer, of course, was that he couldn't. I was living my own story. My family was on their own individual healing journeys, each without a singular timetable or trajectory. All I could do was support them, as they had supported me. I could offer that support with a new freedom now: I'd successfully conquered my most disturbing demons.

CHAPTER 20

Thriving Beyond Surviving: Post-Traumatic Growth

November 2013 (and Beyond)

There's a ton of psychological research being done about post-traumatic growth," said my sister-in-law Caroline. It was Thanksgiving weekend (less than six months after my mindfulness class had ended), and we were sitting at my kitchen table and discussing her work with a veterans' organization.

"What did you just say?" I had never heard these seemingly contradictory words strung together in this way.

"Post-traumatic growth. It's a concept that developed from studies about veterans suffering from post-traumatic stress disorder," Caroline, who has a Ph.d. both in nursing and criminology, explained. "Post-traumatic growth happens when a trauma survivor regains their emotional health and then learns life lessons from it."

I was transfixed. Caroline went on to explain that although post-traumatic stress disorder (PTSD) is frequently referenced in popular culture, most veterans of modern-era combat exhibit some level of post-traumatic growth (PTG): they find personal meaning in trauma, move forward, and grow emotionally.[9] "PTG

9. See <www.researchgate.net/publication/262876138> for more information.

is more common than you'd think, and it's not just for veterans. It's really for anyone who lives through a major crisis," Caroline added.

I felt my shoulders relax as a surge of relief washed over me. I'd thought the tragedy of losing Laura would have destroyed us, *should* have destroyed us. I'd also thought the shock of my own diagnosis would've pushed us over the edge. Yet only a year after my health crisis, our family once again seemed to be doing better than okay, and that's not what seemed normal. That's not what seemed politically correct to admit.

According to Caroline, individuals with the most severe injuries often (and surprisingly) tend to develop an even more positive attitude than those with less serious impairments; instead of becoming bitter or angry, these survivors become more grateful for what they still have and more determined to persevere.[10] That idea immediately rang true for me: after having survived the loss of a child, recovering from brain surgery paled in comparison and had actually increased my motivation. The bigger the challenge, the more determined I'd been to overcome it.

Minutes after Caroline left for the airport, I began searching the Internet for more information on the research of Lawrence G. Calhoun and Richard G. Tedeschi.[11] These two professors at the University of North Carolina, Charlotte had pioneered the first research on PTG in the mid-1990s. The individuals they studied had each suffered a significant stressor (an event that divided their life into a "before" and an "after"), and each had

---

10. See <www.pdhealth.mil/news/blog/post-traumatic-growth-among-ser-vice-members-are-negative-outcomes-only-outcomes> for more information.

11. See <https://ptgi.uncc.edu> for more information and supporting studies.

the potential for experiencing either PTSD or PTG—or a combination of both. A survivor's resilience, the ability to adapt to circumstances beyond their control, determined how well they handled the stress and moved past it. In their work, Calhoun and Tedeschi compared resilience to a muscle that can be strengthened by coping with negative experiences; the more the "resilience muscle" is tested, the stronger it becomes. In other words, tragedy can either destroy you, define you, or determine if and how you will thrive.

As I researched their work further, I learned that most people live through at least one traumatic event, and a significant percentage of survivors experience substantial emotional growth weeks, months, or even years later. I realized that I knew many tales of perseverance and triumph, including the stories of Helen Keller, Christopher Reeve, and Gabrielle Giffords, but I also began reading about everyday people—from many different backgrounds—who experienced PTG without the benefit of celebrity, financial security, strong support networks, or stable childhoods. Throughout my life, I'd underestimated how often adversity strikes, and I'd never understood how others' ability to cope might influence my own. I'd believed that crumbling after trauma was the norm, yet all the material I was now exploring proved me wrong. In a 2013 *Huffington Post* article, professor Calhoun summed up this frequent misconception in one simple sentence. "We are used to expecting the pain and distress, but we may be surprised by the positive life changes."

The more I read about PTG, the more I felt validated. Learning that PTG is a legitimate human reaction to trauma taught me that my family wasn't alone in our resilience. Like so many trauma survivors, we hadn't shaken our fists at God. We'd refused to abandon our family's future well-being and sink into self-pity or fear—merely "treading water" was out of the question. We could count ourselves among those who had not only survived but thrived.

While PTG is common, it's also very personal. From Calhoun and Tedeschi's studies, I learned that not everyone experiences the same extent of emotional growth after trauma, and for some people PTG isn't ever achieved—those who have suffered shouldn't ever be judged or compared to one other. In fact, nonjudgment is PTG's first caveat. PTG also doesn't come with a timetable—it often surfaces over months or years. Emotional growth and ongoing distress are also not mutually exclusive; they often occur simultaneously. Lastly, no amount of progress can erase or make up for the trauma itself. In our lives, just because we learned to be more flexible and compassionate after Laura's death didn't mean we still weren't grieving for her; no emotional growth could ever outweigh the agony of losing Laura.

Even though PTG varies based on the individual and situation—and even though everyone reacts to trauma in their own way—strong physical, mental, and emotional health prior to any adversity all increase the likelihood of responding well. Other traits can also contribute to PTG: overall stability and optimism; the ability to accept what can't be changed; a tendency toward extroversion; a willingness to be vulnerable and authentic; an openness to spirituality; and the ability to infuse some sense of meaning into seemingly senseless events. In that sense, Ron and I were fortunate: pre-trauma, we had our emotional, physical, and financial ducks in a row. We were deeply connected to our community, and we drew strength from Jewish traditions. Our parents had provided us both with stable childhoods, and, as adults, we had their unconditional support to call upon. Our outlook on life is generally positive, and we are both naturally talkative and outgoing. All these factors, and many others, helped us survive through challenges that we once believed were not only inconceivable, but insurmountable.

When Ron and I had trusted our "plow-through" instincts, we'd inadvertently set our family on the road to PTG. By donating Laura's organs—and later by welcoming Trish into our lives—we were keeping Laura's spirit with us and honoring her legacy in the most meaningful way possible. When we sent Sara and Rachel back to school and we returned to our daily schedules so soon after the funeral, we were practicing resilience. By putting our own needs first, we were embracing determination. By accepting our new identities, we were refusing to allow circumstances to define us. By continuing to parent Sara and Rachel with so much energy, we were focusing optimistically on all our futures. By sharing our story—both Laura's story and that of my illness—we were building and strengthening authentic relationships. By twice accepting help, we were showing vulnerability and putting our trust in those who cared about us. And for me, having "stared down" death further solidified my self-confidence.

At the heart of it, our family grew *because* of trauma, not despite it, and during our journey we were blessed with many unexpected, unintended positive outcomes. Perhaps that's not the "right" thing to admit as a parent who lost a child, perhaps that's not the "expected" thing to say as a brain tumor survivor, but it *is* our experience.

While we were in the first years of mourning Laura, I was often told that we were an "inspiration for doing so well," and I was asked—usually in the same breath—how we managed to keep going. Even though the comments were intended kindly, they still unsettled me: how miserable and broken, exactly, were we expected to be?

I felt that same tension after my surgery, as if we were defying society's expectations for a diminished life. In both cases, the stark disparity between others' gloomy predictions and our better-than-anticipated reality was palpable. Were we supposed to stay stuck in our misery forever, to never enjoy our lives again? No. Learning about PTG taught me something else essential: there's room for joy even amid suffering. In fact, embracing that joy is an essential part of growth.

All life experiences are relative. Situations can always be worse, and they can always be better. Comparing trauma, healing, or even the pace and extent of our own recovery to anyone else's dishonors our humanity and ignores our wonderfully imperfect individuality. Trauma and loss are deeply personal, as is our reaction to them, but we can intentionally choose to welcome the happiness we still have, even in our most dismal moments.

While I once wished someone could've given me a clear, step-by-step roadmap on navigating loss and trauma, today I understand that my family's path could only have been forged by us, in our own way. No one else's perspective could've been better than relying on our own gut instincts, mistakes and all. No one else could've possibly understood the love we had—and still have—for Laura. No one else could've known what our family's reliving another too-similar illness was really like. No one else could've fathomed our determination to survive, no one else could ever have taught us *how* to thrive. And today, no matter how crazy it may sound, we still feel fortunate and genuinely hopeful about the future.

My adult life resembles little of the idyllic world I was "promised" as a child, and yet I've grown to understand that the human experience bears little resemblance to perfection. Sara and Rachel, at their young ages, intrinsically understand what it's taken me more than fifty years to learn: Life is not easy or predictable, and sadly no "trauma rules" exist to protect survivors against additional strife. Yet in the end, that's okay—that *has* to be okay. As my mother often says, "It is what it is."

My family and I have learned to live in the paradox of life's negatives and positives: despair and triumph, depression and motivation, heartsickness and healing, devastation and resilience. For anyone who worries about what the future holds—and that seems to be just about everybody—the same can be true.

Epilogue

"Mom, I don't understand why you're writing a book," Rachel teased me one afternoon as I sat at the computer, "because everyone's already heard our story!"

I both laughed and cringed at the truth behind her words. She was right. Not surprisingly, my primal craving to tell our story to friends, family, and anyone else who would listen, morphed into a passion for recording my experiences in this memoir.

Although I'd often longed, when I was younger, to write a book, I didn't believe I would ever have a story worth telling. Little did I know that I would not only end up with a tale worth telling, but one with more tragic, traumatic, and inspirational elements than an editor might recommend including in one manuscript. Writing *Permission to Thrive* has allowed me to preserve my memories—however biased or flawed they might be—for Sara, Rachel, and the generations to come, while also letting me reach out to a wider audience. My hope is that by learning firsthand about our struggles, others will gain faith in their own capacity for resilience and personal growth.

Like others who've struggled with loss and searched for healing and meaning, my mulling, researching, writing, and rewriting have been therapeutic. As time passed, I'd feared my recollection of our experiences and emotions—despite their intensity at the time—would fade. Perhaps they have to some degree, but, for reasons I'm still not able to fully explain, writing about our family's journey and expressing my personal insights have been essential for creating a sense of peace within me.

Above all, this project—which is obviously dedicated to Laura—has provided me with the opportunity, as Laura's mom, to recount her life, express our family's unending love for her, and convey her profound and enduring impact. With this book, I hope a little piece of Laura will touch those who never knew her.

Finishing this memoir has been my bridge to cross, mountain to climb, my cross to bear—or whatever other clichés I've been told *not* to use. Without question, my family's experiences don't represent those of a typical family, and I would more than understand those who have doubts about similarly terrifying traumas ever striking their own lives. Fair enough. Only a small minority of parents will lose a child from a brain tumor—and even fewer will be diagnosed with their own. While our story is extraordinary in many ways, loss and adversity touch everyone, and I believe common threads run through most of life's crises. These threads bind us together, in our common humanity, as we each navigate our hurdles.

Since discovering PTG and the field of positive psychology, I've researched related topics such as grief recovery, resilience, and spirituality. I've spent hundreds of hours viewing our family's story through these lenses, and I've learned just how false, as well as dispiriting, society's expectations about not "bouncing back" from serious hardship can be. The truth is that resilience and PTG aren't just for a lucky few. Most of us can and do move forward, just in our own way and at our own pace.

Our own family's journey was filled with many unexpected events, not the least of which was donating Laura's organs. The resulting cascade of consequences has redefined our lives in the most positive ways possible. That one life-saving decision not only brought Trish into our family, but it has shaped Sara's goals ever since she was a teenager. After her advocacy work in high school, Sara founded SODA (Student Organ Donation Advocates) during her freshman year at Washington University in St. Louis; the club has now expanded to several other campuses. In 2014, and with the help of the BloodCenter of Wisconsin, Trish and our family were featured in a brief educational video, "Laura's Gift of Life," which can be found on YouTube. The video closes with Sara encouraging all viewers to register as organ donors. Today, Sara continues her passion on a volunteer basis while working in healthcare.

As for Rachel, she's on her own path toward achievement. As of this writing, she has just moved to Washington, D.C., to begin her first semester at George Washington University. In the nearly ten years since Laura's death, Rachel has often commented about having faced traumas rarely experienced by those her age. And she's correct. Our crises have unmistakably shaped her personality, but all life's events change us, whether we want them to or not. Although Rachel's childhood was twice disrupted, she still has a remarkably generous, optimistic, and even-keeled personality that will serve her well as she pursues her major in human services and social justice.

Both Rachel and Sara instinctively appreciate the "normal" days, days which others their age most likely take for granted. They also understand that Ron and I treasure them all the more in the absence of their older sister. They know this on a profound level, but it doesn't stop them from joking about my "channeling" Laura's love of fashion when we go shopping together—when sometimes I insist on buying more outfits than either of them has room for in her closet.

Ron still enjoys his career, and he continues to increase his community involvement. With his unique brand of patience, empathy, and support, he continues to be my cynical optimist. I know that, like me, Ron still misses Laura every day. I also know that he shares my all-too-human underlying apprehension: we both understand that our family—even after all we've been through—is no more immune from additional tragedies than anyone else. Life is not fair or equal. Although it may seem like a contradiction, we've learned to accept this uncertainty *and* remain optimistic at heart.

I cannot downplay the significance my twenty-plus years of volunteering has had on our road to healing. The support our family received—practical, emotional, spiritual—far outweighed anything that I'd contributed through my work. Today, I continue to offer my time and resources to the community; I've also begun speaking about post-traumatic growth, personal relationship building, and organ-donor advocacy.

Now that Sara and Rachel have both left home and we've become "empty-nesters," Ron and I are looking forward—as fearlessly as possible—to the next chapter in our lives. While we can't ever know what adversities we'll encounter in the future, we're grounded in knowing that we have the strength and courage to thrive.

Acknowledgments

My long list of thank yous begins with my editor, Erika DeSimone (of Erika's Editing) for her impeccable grammar "nerdiness," her endless patience with my frequent rounds of revisions, and her uncanny ability to see the forest *through* the trees. She helped me intensify my message while refining my voice and respecting our family's personal story.

Thank you also to Hobie and Kathi of Dunn & Associates for developing and designing the cover and jacket. I'm also indebted to Beth Oden for her web-design and marketing expertise.

I'm thankful for the early-stage editing and brainstorming assistance of Priscilla, Ruth B., Peggy, and Maggie. A big thank you also to my friendly "experts": Rabbi Barbara Symons, Dr. Sara Swanson, and nurse Emily Kirchhoefer (formerly of the Wisconsin Donor Network), who have each ensured that I've used the correct terminology when writing about their respective fields.

I cannot imagine where I would be without my family. Thank you to my mom and dad (of blessed memory), and to Ron's parents—who I also call mom and dad—for their unwavering love, and for doing their best to comfort us even as they also were in mourning.

I'm grateful to my sister Karen and brother Steven for their love, and particularly for their patience as they stayed overnight with me in the hospital and weathered my incessant post-op demands and ramblings. I also owe their spouses a sincere thanks—to Alan for his constant kindness and to Caroline for introducing me to the inspirational concept of post-traumatic growth. For so many reasons, I also want to express my appreciation to Ron's sister Amy and her husband Jack, who drove four hours to Milwaukee from their home in Iowa on more than a few occasions, as well as to Ron's older brother Neal. Perhaps more than anything else, Ron and I appreciate how all of our siblings have nurtured strong first-cousin relationships between our daughters and their children. We treasure all our nieces and nephews as well as their respective partners: Ed and Ashley, Lisa and Andrew, Sam, Melissa and Aaron, Ellen, Jason, Adam, Catherine, and Josh. We love you!

When it comes to my friends, I'm at a loss to convey the impact of their healing powers and truly vital assistance. They are my superheroes! A huge thank you to those who coordinated and prepared dinners for our family when I was unable; to my friends who answered my tearful calls; to my neighbors who welcomed me into their homes at all hours of the day and night; to so many in the community who patiently listened while remarkably never judging my actions; to our college friends who traveled long distances to be with us during our darkest days; to those who sat with me through my recovery; and especially to those who took good care of Sara and Rachel when Ron and I—on two different occasions—were in ultra-crisis mode. You are each engraved on my heart.

"Embraced by the community" isn't a phrase I ever expected to utter so sincerely and passionately, yet Milwaukee's Jewish community—including our rabbi and cantor at Congregation Shalom—twice rallied around us. I'm especially thankful for those at the Milwaukee Jewish Federation, the Harry & Rose Samson Family Jewish Community Center, National Council of Jewish Women–Milwaukee Section, and COA Youth & Family Services, including the HIPPY Program. Truly, we are stronger together.

Laura's friends will forever be our family's friends. In particular, we appreciate Laura's BBYO youth group members for their outpouring of heartfelt condolences, their passion for honoring her memory, and for welcoming Sara and Rachel once they each became old enough for membership. Also, I'd like to thank BBYO's director Rachael B., without whom we never would have connected with the Wolfe family or formed the Laura Miller Memorial Team for the annual "Run with Wolfes" event.

As for Trish, what can I say? We're still inspired by her courageous and kind spirit, and we're beyond grateful to her husband Gary and her family for their willingness to welcome us into their lives. We couldn't have wished for a better person to carry on Laura's legacy.

If not for my neurosurgeon and the skilled team of neuro-interventional radiologists at Froedtert Hospital, I wouldn't have lived to write this memoir; I'm forever indebted to them. And, I don't want to overlook the critical role my therapist Laurie played in encouraging us to trust our instincts.

Words escape me when I think about Sara and Rachel and their compassion and resilience. They stayed strong while I openly grieved, then cared for me through my own illness for more months than I'd like to admit. Their hugs alone saw me through many challenging days.

For more than thirty years, I've been truly blessed to have Ron as my husband and my True North. He's always ready to help when I need it, and he pushes me to be better than I ever could be on my own. ("I found a good one," is what I simply tell our daughters.) Even though Ron is a relatively private person, he patiently supported me as I wrote this memoir. He understands the power of our story and my need to share our family's experiences, and, above all, he wants what's best for me. There are no words to express my love and appreciation.

My Suggested Reading List

During my journey to post-traumatic growth, and while writing *Permission to Thrive*, I've read many books on grief, personal relationships, mindfulness, and resilience. What follows is a list of the titles that I've found most relevant, insightful, and encouraging. I hope they help you on your own path of self-awareness and healing.

Being Mortal: Medicine and What Matters in the End, by Atul Gawande

Bouncing Forward: The Art and Science of Cultivating Resilience, by Michaela Haas

Click: The Forces Behind How We Fully Engage with People, Work, and Everything We Do, by Ori Brafman and Rom Brafman

Handbook of Posttraumatic Growth: Research and Practice, by Lawrence G. Calhoun and Richard G. Tedeschi

The Miracle of Mindfulness: An Introduction to the Practice of Meditation, by Thich Nhat Hanh

My Stroke of Insight: A Brain Scientist's Personal Journey, by Jill Bolte Taylor

The Other Side of Sadness: What the New Science of Bereavement Tells Us about Life after Loss, by George A. Bonanno

Resilience: The Science of Mastering Life's Greatest Challenges, by Steven M. Southwick and Dennis S. Charney

The Road to Resilience: From Chaos to Celebration, by Sherri Mandell

The Scalpel and the Soul: Encounters with Surgery, the Supernatural, and the Healing Power of Hope, by Allan J. Hamilton

Man's Search for Meaning, by Viktor E. Frankl

Supersurvivors: The Surprising Link Between Suffering and Success, by David B. Feldman and Lee Daniel Kravetz

There Is No Good Card for This: What to Say and Do When Life Is Scary, Awful, and Unfair to People You Love, by Kelsey Crowe and Emily McDowell

Upside: The New Science of Post-Traumatic Growth, by Jim Rendon

What Doesn't Kill Us: The New Psychology of Posttraumatic Growth, by Stephen Joseph

When Bad Things Happen to Good People, by Harold S. Kushner

Reader's Guide:
Questions and Topics for
Discussion

1. The title of this book, "Permission to Thrive," speaks to allowing ourselves to feel and behave in the way which feels right for a given situation, especially during times of crisis. How does this concept play a role in the journey of Susan and her family? Did any of their choices surprise you or make you feel uncomfortable? If so, why?

2. Organ donation stories are more often told from the perspective of the organ recipient than the donor family, while *Permission* shows us both sides. What details about the two families' stories stood out to you? Have you and your family discussed your own views on organ donation? What parts of the donation process would you like to learn more about?

3. Throughout this book, Susan refers to Jewish traditions, including those for mourning, as well as her religion's beliefs about organ donation. In what ways, if any, have your own religious traditions helped you weather life's challenges?

4. Susan speaks extensively about her gratitude for the support her friends, family, and community offered as she and her family faced two separate crises. How did Susan's volunteering within her community play a part in nurturing, and then

activating, this essential support system? What role does community play in your own life?

5. Susan and her family used two websites, CaringBridge and Lotsa Helping Hands, to reach out to friends and family for help, and many people—from all areas of their lives—answered the call. How have you offered your support to others when they needed it?

6. In chapter ten, Susan states that many believed her marriage to Ron would be in jeopardy specifically because they lost a child. In response, she cites research to debunk this widely-held myth. How did Ron and Susan focus on their relationship including their shared role as parents, as they faced their loss? What factors do you believe impact the health of a partnership following traumatic events?

7. Susan tells us that in his book, *The Other Side of Sadness*, author George A. Bonanno asserts that Western society does not do well with death. After reading *Permission*, what specific lessons have you learned about reaching out to those in mourning? When we interact with those who are grieving, how can we express more empathy than pity?

8. Susan discusses the vulnerabilities intrinsic to grieving and to recovering from an illness, as well as the human need to rely on others during times of adversity. When have you had to rely on others for help and how did it make you feel? What specific types of support have you found to be the most helpful and necessary when going through an especially trying time?

9. In the moments after learning about her own brain tumor, Susan wonders why she and her family must face yet another

major crisis—why they weren't given a "get out of jail free card." Why do we so often believe that surviving one crisis somehow protects us from additional strife? What purpose can be found in this hopeful thinking?

10. Were you shocked at the change in Susan's behavior as she recovered from her surgery? What positive emotional growth did she experience during this time? What were the negatives she and her family experienced?

11. What role did mindfulness play in Susan's recovery after her surgery? Were you surprised at her willingness to explore this alternative approach to healing? How did practicing mindfulness help Susan to regain her own health, and how did it help her finally come to terms with Laura's death?

12. Susan was inspired to write this book after learning about the positive-psychological concept of post-traumatic growth (PTG). In your life, what, if any, aspects of PTG have you experienced? What personality traits do you believe help or hinder emotional growth following trauma? How can we better prepare ourselves for unexpected adversity?

13. What are PTG's main caveats? If a survivor does not experience PTG after a trauma, how can we still offer support without being judgmental?

14. Resilience is a theme throughout this book. How do you define *resilience*, and how do you compare it to post-traumatic growth? How are they similar? How do they differ?

15. Overall, what was your main takeaway from *Permission*? How can you incorporate that understanding into your everyday life?

About the Author

Susan Angel Miller is a career volunteer who has held leadership positions at the National Council of Jewish Women–Milwaukee Section, the Harry & Rose Samson Family Jewish Community Center, and the Milwaukee Jewish Federation. She works with other Milwaukee nonprofits such as HIPPY (Home Instruction for Parents of Preschool Youngsters), the Wisconsin Donor Network (part of the Versiti Network), and SODA (Student Organ Donation Advocates). Susan participates in an annual memorial walk in honor of her daughter Laura, and she raises contributions for the Laura Miller Fund at the Jewish Community Foundation. She also leads presentations on post-traumatic growth, personal relationship building skills, and organ donor advocacy.

Susan received her undergraduate degree in political science from the University of Michigan and her MBA from Loyola University in Chicago. She began her career as a marketing consultant to community banks before devoting her skills full-time to nonprofit work, including strategic planning, community outreach, and mentoring projects.

She is married to her exceptionally supportive and resilient husband Ron; they are the proud parents of Sara, Rachel, and their forever-beloved Laura.

If you know others who are facing significant challenges and who might benefit from reading about our family's experiences, please share this book with them and consider posting a review on Amazon.com, to enable our story to reach more people.

All proceeds from book sales will be donated to the Laura Miller Donor-Advised Fund at the Jewish Community Foundation of the Milwaukee Jewish Federation. Monies will fund brain cancer research and organ donation awareness.

For more information or to make a donation, please go to SusanAngelMiller.com